HITTIN' THE TRAIL: WISCONSIN

Day Hiking Trails of the
Chippewa Valley

By Rob Bignell

Atiswinic Press · Ojai, Calif.

DAY HIKING TRAILS OF THE CHIPPEWA VALLEY

A GUIDEBOOK IN THE
HITTIN' THE TRAIL: WISCONSIN SERIES

Copyright Rob Bignell, 2016

Atiswinic Press
Ojai, Calif. 93023
dayhikingtrails.wordpress.com

ISBN 978-0-9961625-4-8

Cover design by Rob Bignell
Cover photo of Chippewa River at Brunet Island State Park
All interior photos by Rob Bignell

Manufactured in the United States of America
First printing April 2016

For Kieran

Table of Contents

Introduction

Imagine a place where you can walk beneath rare giant conifers and over nearly 2 billion-year-old rock, where you can traipse the scenic routes of old railroad lines along majestic rivers that feed the Mississippi, where you can whistle as passing rustic trout streams and turtle ponds or pause in reverent silence by ancient effigy mounds. The place is real: It's called the Chippewa Valley.

Located along the Chippewa River in west-central Wisconsin, the valley is an outdoor recreational paradise. Cross-country skiers, snowmobilers and snowshoers zip across trails while ice fisherman dot frozen lakes each winter. Those longing to see colorful leaves and to pick fresh apples drive along its winding river valleys come autumn. And every summer, hikers and bicyclists alike explore its many woodlands, historic sites, and geological wonders.

The Chippewa River stretches 183 miles across Wisconsin. Originally the term "Chippewa Valley" referred to the Chippewa River watershed but in the public's eye soon came to more narrowly mean the Eau Claire-Chippewa Falls metro area. As the nearby communities of Menomonie and Durand grew increasingly intertwined economically with that metro area, the term has broadened to include them, which better encompasses but still offers an incomplete overlay of the Chippewa River watershed. For the purposes of this book, the Chippewa Valley includes all of Eau Claire, Chippewa, and Dunn counties and eastern Pepin County.

Geology

While rock can be found in the Chippewa Valley that dates to at least 1.85 billion years, most of the area's bedrock was formed much later. Prior to 545 million years ago, the four counties making up what is now the river valley sat off the edge of the North American continent near the equator. Over the next 50 million years, the bedrock for most of Eau Claire and Chippewa counties formed in the Cambrian period and then in the 50 million years following, during the Ordovician, the bedrock for Dunn and Pepin counties developed. Most of the sandstone above this bedrock is visible in road cuts and where the Chippewa and Eau Claire rivers have carved through it.

Much of the geological record between 443 million and 1.8 million years ago has disappeared from the Chippewa Valley. During that time, the area probably lay under a sea for several million years with the rest lost to erosion, both from everyday causes such as rain and wind and from the glaciers that swept through the area.

Much of the landscape today in the Chippewa Valley is shaped by the last ice age. The Chippewa River sits in a wide canyon, formed more than 18,000 years ago when ice sheets began to melt and retreat in this area of Wisconsin. As the glaciers' advance stopped in northern Chippewa County, sediment brought from those melting ice sheets formed a thin layer over much of the area's existing bedrock. How the melting ice molded the Chippewa Valley – the Chippewa River itself was a major channel for the meltwater flowing into the Mississippi River – is a complex story that varies across the region.

Geography

The Chippewa River runs about 183 miles from northern Wisconsin into the Mississippi River, where sediment helps back up the river and forms Lake Pepin. Only the Chippewa River's lower 50 miles from the Mississippi River northward is navigable.

About half of Chippewa County – the northeast corner – sits in the Northern Highlands. The site of an ancient mountain range, it is now a hilly region with virtually no lakes or wetlands. It mostly belongs to the North Central Forest ecological zone.

Most of Dunn County, the southwestern half of Chippewa County, and the northern and eastern portion of Eau Claire County, are in the Central Plain. Half-a-billion years ago, much of this area was a coastal plain bordering a sea. It has since been uplifted hundreds of feet with erosion over the millennia and the most recent ice ages reducing the terrain to a fairly flat surface. Ecologically, it's part of the Western Coulee and Ridges area.

The western edges of Dunn County, much of Pepin County, and the southeastern portion of Eau Claire County is part of the Western Upland. A system of ridges and valleys make up the area around the Chippewa and Mississippi rivers. This region ecologically also belongs to the Western Coulee and Ridges area.

History

Before Europeans arrived, the Dakota Sioux dominated the Chippewa Valley, and remnants of their presence via burial mounds still can be found. The first Euro-Americans to explore the region were the French, and Lake Pepin – which the Chippewa River forms by dumping sediment into the Mississippi River – likely was named for two of those adventurers, the brothers Pierre Pepin and Jean Pepin du Cardonnets. These explorers primarily sought a water passageway through North America to the Pacific Ocean, and portages from the Great Lakes to the Mississippi River brought them to the Chippewa River Valley.

In the late 1600s, Frenchman Nicholas Perrot brashly claimed all lands west of the Great Lakes for his king, and during the next century France dominated mining, trading and trapping in the region. Archeological evidence indicates several French trading posts existed on Lake Pepin during the 1700s.

With the growth of the American colonies on the East Coast, Native American tribes migrated west, leading to conflicts with the already existing Indian nations there. Among them was the pressing of the Ojibwa in northern Wisconsin into Dakota Sioux territory. For Euro-Americans, this raised the value of the Chippewa River as a route between Lake Superior and the Mississippi River to avoid being caught up in tribal tensions.

Great Britain ended French dominance in the area during the French and Indian War of 1754-63, and when the American colonies gained independence, they claimed the area as part of the Northwest Territories. The Chippewa River garnered its name from an Anglicization of "Ojibwa," the name for the native American tribe who controlled much of the upper Chippewa Valley during the early 1800s.

Wisconsin became a state in 1846, but most of the population lived in the southern portion near the Illinois border. The Chippewa River served as a major route to the great pineries of the north as settlers arrived in the area during the next five decades. The river also was the main waterway for bringing felled logs to sawmills in Chippewa Falls and Eau Claire and then exporting the cut lumber via the Mississippi River to other parts of the rapidly growing United States.

Two of the most famous children's stories of pioneers – those of Laura Ingalls Wilder and Caddie Woodlawn – both have their origins in the Chippewa Valley. "Little House in the Big Woods," the first in the Laura Ingalls Wilder series, is set north of Pepin, while the Caddie Woodlawn tales took place south of Menomonie.

With the great forests logged off and arrival of the railroads, agriculture quickly became the mainstay of communities throughout the Chippewa Valley. Dairy farming in particular prevailed with manufacturing springing up in the region's larger cities.

Today, hiking trails in the area tend to offer glimpses of the area's natural beauty that existed before the logging industry cleared the forests. A number of trails honor the region's history – from burial mounds to the great railroads.

Communities

Several small cities and villages can be found in the Chippewa Valley. Most of those communities have longed served as agricultural centers, but the region's four dominant towns also became manufacturing, education or government hubs. Not surprisingly, those four all are on the region's three major rivers.

Eau Claire, with a population of nearly 70,000, sits at the confluence of the Chippewa and Eau Claire rivers. At one time, this was the nation's lumber capital, but that role gave way to industry in the 20th century. Today, it's best known as the home of the University of Wisconsin-Eau Claire and as a regional government and retail center. Recent efforts to make the city trail-friendly has led to a number of hiking opportunities here, especially downtown and on the **Chippewa River State Trail**.

Menomonie, to the west, is the valley's second most populous city at around 16,500. The Red Cedar River, a major tributary to the Chippewa River, runs through town. It is home of the University of Wisconsin-Stout and offers several excellent trails, most notably the **Red Cedar State Trail**.

Chippewa Falls, the valley's third largest city at about 14,000, also is on the Chippewa River and shares a similar lumbering and manufacturing legacy as Eau Claire to the south. Today, it is headquarters for the original Cray Research and home of the Jacob Leinenkugel Brewing Company. The southern end of the **Old Abe Trail** is located here; a couple of other good trails also can be found in Irvine Park.

Though smaller than a couple of other cities in the valley – specifically Altoona and Bloomer – Durand with 2000 people is Pepin County's seat of government. It is downstream from Eau Claire on the Chippewa River, and the **Chippewa River State Trail's** southern terminus is here.

Attractions

The Chippewa Valley boasts a number of parks and trails ideal for hiking.

Highlighting those attractions are two state parks. **Brunet Island State Park** covers 1300 acres on the Chippewa River and boasts several quiet lagoons. To the south, **Lake Wissota State Park** spans over a thousand acres along a reservoir on the Chippewa.

Several minor state public areas as well as county and city parks can be found in the region. Two of them particularly stand out. The **Chippewa Moraine State Recreation Area** at more than 3000 acres in size preserves several unique landforms created during the last ice age. **Hoffman Hills Recreation Area** covers a little more than 700 acres and includes an observation tower at its highest point.

Each of the Chippewa Valley's three largest cities operate sizeable parks. Chippewa Falls' **Irvine Park** includes a zoo, cave and walk along a creek. Eau Claire's **Carson Park** offers historical museums and a trail near the Chippewa River. Menomonie's **Wakanda Park** sits on Lake Menomin and adjoins a game park with nature trail.

Four lengthy trails crisscross the valley. The **Chippewa River State Trail** runs 26 miles along its namesake from Durand to the Lake Hallie area north of Eau Claire. The **Old**

Abe State Trail heads 19.5 miles along the Chippewa River from Chippewa Falls to Brunet Island State Park. The **Red Cedar State Trail** hugs the Red Cedar River for 14.5 miles from Menomonie to northeast of Durand. Each of those three trails were built on old railroad grades. A fourth route, the **Ice Age National Scenic Trail**, marks the farthest advance of glaciers in the last ice age, and runs for 23 miles in Chippewa County, from north of Stanley to northeast of New Auburn.

When to Visit

The best months to day hike the Chippewa Valley are May through September. Depending on the year, April and October also can be pleasant.

As with the rest of the Upper Midwest, summers are humid, especially July and August. Rain can occur during the afternoon even when the morning is sunny, so always check the weather forecast before heading out.

November through March usually is too cold for day hiking. Once snow falls, trails typically are used for cross-country skiing, snowmobiling or snowshoeing. In early spring, trails often are muddy thanks to snowmelt and rainfall.

How to Get There

Several major highways lead to and cross the Chippewa Valley.

From the Minneapolis-St. Paul area, take Interstate 94 east. Trails in Dunn and Pepin county trails can be accessed by exiting on Wis. Hwy. 25, while many trails in Eau Claire and Chippewa counties can be reached by exiting onto U.S. Hwy. 53 or U.S. Hwy 12.

From northern Wisconsin and Minnesota, take Hwy. 53 south into Chippewa County. Continue south into Eau Claire County or take Wis. Hwy. 29 west to Dunn County.

From southern Minnesota and Iowa, either Interstate 35 can be taken north to Minneapolis-St. Paul and then I-94 east into Dunn and Eau Claire counties or U.S. Hwy. 63 can be taken north to I-94, which then is traveled east.

From eastern Wisconsin, either U.S. Hwy. 10 or Hwy. 29 can be driven east to I-94.

From the Upper Peninsula, take U.S. Hwy. 8 west then Hwy. 53 south.

From southern Wisconsin and Illinois, head north on I-94 into Eau Claire County.

Maps

One thing you won't find in this guidebook is maps. To properly prepare for any hike, you should examine maps before hitting the trail and bring them with you (See the Special Section for more.). No guidebook can reproduce a map as well as the satellite pictures or topographical maps that you can find online for free. To that end, a companion website (*dayhikingtrails.wordpress.com/trail-maps*) to this book offers a variety of printable maps for each listed trail.

Featured Trails

The Chippewa Valley consists of four counties that the Chippewa River runs through. Chippewa County makes up the northeast corner, Eau Claire County the east-central section, Dunn County the northwest and west-central area, and Pepin County the southern portion. More than 100 hiking trails can be found on public lands in the region.

Chippewa County

C hippewa County is prime day hiking country. Two state parks, a state recreation area, the Ice Age National Scenic Trail, the Old Abe State Trail, an impressive city park in Chippewa Falls, and several smaller county and city parks all can be found there. Much of the county's northern portion is a showcase for moraines, kettle lakes and other post-ice age features. The Chippewa River splits the county in half, running diagonally northeast to southwest. Trails in this section are listed roughly northwest to southeast.

Circle Trail
Chippewa Moraine State Recreation Area and Ice Age National Scientific Reserve

Day hikers can wind their way through ancient lakes formed by melting glaciers on the Circle Trail.

The trail at the Chippewa Moraine State Recreation Area and Ice Age National Scientific Reserve forms a 4.5-mile loop. As the Recreation Area is part of the Ice Age National Scientific Reserve, Federal passes are honored.

To reach the trailhead, from U.S. Hwy. 53 in New Auburn, go east on County Road M. The rec area is in about 7 miles; watch for signs for the David R. Obey Ice Age Interpretive Center, which is on the left/north.

The interpretive center is a good spot to start the hike. It offers displays explaining how the area was formed by glaciers as well as on cultural and natural history. Kids visiting the center can feed a bug to a fish, pet a turtle, dig for fossils, and even hold a snake.

From the interpretive center, head northwest on the Circle Trail. It's a narrow path of packed dirt through forest with plenty of benches for resting along the way.

In short order, the path passes a pond. This part of the Cir-cle Trail is a segment of the Ice Age National Scenic Trail. Payne Lake appears next on the left.

The many ponds and lakes the trail weaves past were cre-ated rather recently on geological timescales. About 14,000 years ago, glaciers covered this area to roughly a mile south of the interpretive center. As the glacier melted, sand, gravel and other rock were left amid massive chunks of ice; when new, temporary glaciers moved to cover the melt area, they pushed the debris together into hill-shaped piles and natural dams. The result was a 10-mile wide moraine and a series of irregularly shaped lakes and ponds amid plains and mounds.

Next, the trail heads between North Shattuck Lake (on the left/south) and North of North Shattuck Lake (on the right/ north). These and the other waterbodies on the moraine con-sist of melted glacial water trapped amid the debris.

The Ice Age Trail separates as it heads west into the North of North Shattuck Lake State Natural Area. The state natural area and this section of the recreational area are popular among birds during the spring migration. Among those that can be spotted here are American redstarts, eastern wood-pewees, scarlet tanagers, woodpeckers (both hairy and red-headed), and yellow-throated vireos.

Horseshoe Lake next appears on the right/west. This puts you on the loop's western side, where you'll head between two ponds.

While spring and summer make for spectacular bird-watching across the moraine, early autumn also is a great time to visit as lily pads bloom on the ponds and bullfrogs come out and croak in full force. White-tailed deer fawns also are venturing out and can be more easily spotted grazing with their mothers.

Next, the trail crosses County Road M, placing you 1.4 miles from the trailhead. For those needing to walk a shorter distance, this marks a good place to turn back for a 2.8-mile round trip hike.

If continuing on, Jeanstow Lake next appears to the left/east. The trail then curves and begins the loop's southern side.

After passing three ponds, the trail reaches the southeastern shores of South Shattuck Lake on the left/north. At 63 acres, South Shattuck is the largest of the lakes along the Circle Trail. It reaches a depth of 39 feet, and largemouth bass are common in it.

Once beyond South Shattuck Lake, the trail passes another pond on the left then crosses a narrow point in another one. As the trail begins the western side of its loop, it rejoins the Ice Age Trail; at that junction, continue north.

The trail passes yet another pond on the right/east then crosses County Road M a second time. The junction is 3.92 miles from the trailhead. Upon doing so, the trail begins the loop's north side.

The final legs consist of passing a pond on the right/northeast, then heading between two ponds. From there, the trail curves south with a new pond on right/west. After that, you'll arrive back at the interpretive center and parking lot.

Good news for dog owners: Fido and Queenie are allowed off leash on the trail but not in the yards at the interpretive center or in the picnic areas.

Other Chippewa Moraine Recreation Area Trails

• **Dry Lake Trail** – The 1.8-mile loop passes five ponds. It starts near the interpretive center.

• **Ice Age National Scenic Trail segment** – The 1200-mile statewide trail runs roughly where the glacier reached its farthest southern advance during the last ice age. It cuts east-west through the recreation area. From the interpretive center, access it via the Circle Loop.

- **Mammoth Nature Trail** –The 0.75-mile loop passes three ponds. It also starts near the interpretive center.

Ice Age National Scenic Trail, Deer Fly Trail Area segment
Chippewa County Forest

Day hikers can enjoy a walk along the famous Ice Age National Scenic Trail in northern Chippewa County.

More than 20 of the trail's proposed 1200 miles rambles through the county. A particularly good county segment to hike is this 2-miles round-trip in the Chippewa County Forest's Deer Fly Trail area.

To reach this segment, from Bloomer, drive east on Wis. Hwy. 64. Turn left/north onto County Road E then left/north on 180th Street. This road curves west to become 205th Avenue and then north to become 175th Street. When the road turns west and becomes 225th Avenue, head right/north on Hay Meadow Flowage Trail (a road). Then go right/northeast onto the gravel Deer Fly Trail. When the narrow Ice Age Trail crosses the road, park on the shoulder (If you pass the junction with High Ridge Trail road, you've gone too far).

The trail meanders through a mixed hardwood forest. Be careful not to turn off onto crossing logging trails, which will be much wider than the Ice Age Trail. Yellow blazes mark the main trail.

Statewide, the trail roughly marks the advance of glaciers during the last ice age. Those glaciers entirely shaped the terrain throughout the area.

While 11,000 years ago ice towered high above the ground, today the area consists mainly of tag alder swamps, swamp conifers, swamp hardwoods or a mixture of these.

The upland areas, however, consist of aspen, oak or northern hardwoods.

When the trail passes wetlands in about a half-mile, you're close to Birch Creek. The trail largely parallels the stream until veering southwest to the Harwood Lakes.

Along the trail, you'll likely spot deep ruts. They are a testament to man's impact on Mother Nature, for they date to the late 1800s when sled runners pulled by horse teams hauled large loads of white pine logs out of this forest.

The Deer Fly Trail area is fairly secluded, so you won't likely see other hikers out here except maybe on weekends. The Chippewa County Forest covers 33,653-acres, and the Deer Fly area makes up about a quarter of that at 8,589 acres.

About a mile from the trailhead, the trail crosses a narrow spot in the widening creek via a log corduroy. These are logs sand-covered logs that were placed perpendicular to roads that crossed swampy areas. While an improvement over muddy roads, they still made for a bumpy ride and when loose logs shifted could injure horses.

The crossing marks a good point to turn back.

River Road Ski Trail
Harold Walters Memorial Forest

Families can hike rolling, wooded terrain alongside the Chippewa River on the River Road Ski Trail near Cornell.

The 3.5-mile cross country trail rambles through the 270-acre Harold Walters Memorial Forest and can be hiked when snow isn't on the ground. A segment of the trail with the gentlest terrain changes runs about 2.1-miles round trip and offers some views of the river.

To reach the trailhead, from Wis. Hwy 178 in Cornell, drive north on County Road CC. In 2.2 miles, turn right/ northeast onto 239th Avenue; a parking lot is on the road's left/west side.

From the parking lot, go around the gate on the trail that heads northwest. At the first junction, turn right/northeast.

The trail generally heads through a mixed hardwoods forest. This habitat is perfect for the white-tailed deer, which often grazes on agricultural fields at the edge of woodlands.

Wisconsin's official wildlife animal, white-tailed deer are quite common across the state. They can grow up to three-feet high at the shoulder and weigh up to 200 pounds.

Fawns usually are born in May and June, so a great time to hike this trail is late summer when mothers bring out their young. Newborns typically remain low in the grass, and their reddish brown coats with white spots makes for perfect camouflage.

Should you spot a deer, unless it is in the distance or freezes, don't expect to see it for long. Despite long skinny legs, they can run up to 40 miles per hour, jump nine feet high (allowing them to clear almost any fence), and can swim about 13 miles per hour. When broad jumping, they can leap up to 30 feet in a single bound.

The trail parallels the Chippewa River, which runs for 183 miles, rising out of Lake Chippewa in Sawyer County, and flows into the Mississippi River. Where the two rivers meet, the sediment backs up the Mississippi to form Lake Pepin. This trail moves away from the northern tip of the Cornell Flowage, a section of the Chippewa.

In 0.4 miles from trailhead, the route reaches junction 1; go right/east. Within 200 feet, you'll come to junction 2; continue going straight/east.

From there, the trail heads up a steep hill, offering vistas of the Chippewa below. It's particularly scenic in autumn when the leaves of the forest's northern hardwoods turn color and the understory clears away to give views of the blue river.

After walking 0.2 miles, go right/northeast at junction 3. In 0.4 miles at junction 6, turn back, retracing your steps to the parking lot.

Jean Brunet Nature Trail
Brunet Island State Park

Day hikers can experience a river island full of giant conifers on the Jean Brunet Nature Trail near Cornell.

The 1.5-mile round trip trail sits in Brunet Island State Park. The park's heart and its developed sections mostly sit on an island at the confluence of Chippewa and Fisher rivers. Of the route described here, the self-guided nature trail makes up a little more than half of the walk.

To reach the park, from Cornell, go west on Wis. Hwy. 64/ Bridge Street. Turn right/north on Park Road, which leads to the park entrance. Follow the park road over the river and onto the island. Turn at the first left onto the one-way road and park at the boat landing.

From the boat landing, take Pine Trail west, crossing the park road. You'll walk through the southern edge of the state's North Central Forest landscape, which in large part is synonymous with the Wisconsin Northwoods. Here Northern hardwoods grow atop sediment left by glaciers at the end of the last ice age.

Upon coming to the Y in the trail, go right/northwest, continuing on Pine Trail.

You'll likely see whitetail deer or signs of them along the way. The deer are ubiquitous on the island and have radically altered the landscape by feeding on young hemlocks trees that once filled the terrain. The decimation of hemlocks and other native species likely means that red pine and spruce will cover the island in years to come. Efforts are underway by park officials, however, to protect and rejuvenate native species.

After the trail crosses the park road, you'll come to another Y. Go left/north on it; you're a third of the way through the walk and officially on the Jean Brunet Nature Trail – though you're not exactly following the trail from its official starting point, which is near the bridge connecting the island to the mainland.

Deer aren't the only wildlife on the island. Chipmunks, fox, porcupine, raccoons, skunks, squirrels, and woodchucks also call the island home while beaver, otter, mink and muskrat can be seen in the surrounding river channels.

Birds also reside on the islands, especially during spring and fall migrations. Year around, eagles and osprey usually can spotted flying overhead while at night owls can be heard hooting. A healthy-sized population of grouse live in the island's brush.

Even if you don't spot any wildlife, you're certain to see gigantic hemlocks growing along the nature trail. Most of these trees are extremely old, survivors from a day when predators were around to control the deer population.

The trail quickly comes to the river shore and loops about the island's northern edge. Watch for great blue herons that sometimes race in the backwaters.

The park and trail is named for Jean Brunet, who came to the United States from France in the early 1800s. In 1828, he moved to what is now Chippewa Falls and then shortly thereafter to what is now the Cornell area, where he established a trading post, operated a ferry service, and built a dam. Northern States Power Company gave the island to the state in 1936, and it became a park four years later.

The loop forms more of a triangle than a circle with its bottom leg paralleling the park road. Once you've completed the loop, retrace our steps on the Pine Trail back to the park-parking lot.

A 500-foot segment of the trail is handicap accessible with limited parking at the trailhead near the main bridge.

Other Brunet Island State Park Trails

• **Ice Age National Scenic Trail segment** – About 2 miles of the 1200-mile trail crosses the park's sparsely visited west side. Park at the trailhead off of County Road Z west of County Road CC and hike west then north to the trailhead at County Road CC.

• **Nordic Trail** – The 4.3-mile loop in the park's eastern section crosses a variety of post-glacier terrain and for part of the way parallels the scenic Fisher River. Start from the lot at the park headquarters.

• **Old Abe State Trail** – The northern end of the 14-mile trail starts at the park's dumping station and runs south alongside Park Road into Cornell. Use the lot at the park headquarters.

• **Pine Trail** – This 0.6 mile consists of two forks in a red (Norway) pine plantation at the island's center. Park at the boat landing off of 255th Street south of Park Road.

• **Spruce Trail** – The 0.33-mile trail connects a boat landing and boat landing, running alongside a back channel of the Chippewa River. Park at the same lot as for the Pine Trail.

• **Timber Trail** – Mature hemlocks and young aspen stands line the 0.6-mile route that runs between the swimming beach and the North Camp Area. Park at the lot for the fishing pier.

Old Abe State Trail segment

Day hikers can enjoy a walk alongside a Chippewa River reservoir on the Old Abe State Trail.

A former rail line, the 20-mile trail links Chippewa County's two state parks – Brunet Island in Cornell and Lake Wissota near Chippewa Falls. It winds through farmland and forests, past historical sites, and along the Chippewa River shoreline. Though a bicycle trail, it also is open to hikers.

A pleasant 6-mile round trip segment of the trail to day hike is near Jim Falls. To reach the trailhead, in downtown Jim Falls look for the trail parking lot off of County Road S between Barber Drive and 139th Avenue. An access trail heads southeast from the lot to the trail.

Head north on the Old Abe; houses and a county highway sit between the trail and Chippewa River if you go south. While the same is true as heading north through Jim Falls, the built-up area gives way to countryside upon crossing County Road S.

Once north of the county road, the trail passes a transmission substation that pulls power from the hydroelectric dam on the Chippewa River to the east. In short order, the trail comes alongside Old Abe Lake (Some maps refer to it as the "Old Abe Flowage."), a reservoir created by two dams. The first backs up a side channel of the Chippewa Riv-er at County Roads S and Y while the other is farther north on the main channel. The Chippewa River's main channel ram-bles across several cascades.

As the lake narrows, the surrounding land grows swampier. On the opposite shoreline, bluffs rise over the lake and river, each autumn offering a scenic backdrop of harvest colors.

Flat and wide, the Old Abe Trail is a former Chicago and Northwestern rail line. The trail is named for the eagle that served as mascot of the 8th Wisconsin Volunteer Infantry Regiment during the Civil War. Soldiers purchased the eagle from a tavern owner in Jim Falls and took it into many battles across the South.

A good spot to turn back is about three miles into the hike, just after the trail curves northeast toward the 2 o'clock position (with north at noon). Following the spring snow melt, the water can be high here, and the elevated trail forms a causeway over a finger of the lake.

Alternately, you can continue north to Cobban, which at five miles from Jim Falls makes for a great point-to-point trail in which someone picks you up at your destination. Just before arriving, the trail crosses another causeway over the river's side.

Other trailheads for the Old Abe include:

• **Lake Wissota** – A lot is off of Elks Club Road immediately west of the County Roads S and O intersection.

• **Cornell** – Park at the Cornell City and Visitors Center off of Wis. Hwy. 64 west of Park Road.

• **Brunet Island State Park** – The trail runs south from the park headquarters' lot on Park Road.

South Loop
Hickory Ridge Recreation Area

Day hikers can enjoy a pleasant walk around several placid lakes and ponds on the South Loop at the Hickory Ridge Recreational Area east of Bloomer.

Though primarily cross-country skiing trails, the series of stacked loops can be hiked during the other seasons. The South Loop, a 3.1-miles round trip lollipop, is a good choice as it's a little flatter than the other two routes on site.

To reach the trailhead, from Bloomer head west on Wis. Hwy. 64. Go left/north onto County Road AA then right/east onto 226th Avenue, which as veering south naturally becomes 225th Avenue (aka Bob Lake Road). The parking lot is on the north side of the road just east of Big Buck Lake.

The trail runs north from the lot, curving around a wet meadow known locally as the "Great Swamp." It then passes the eastern side of Horseshoe Lake, which is on the trail's west side. At 19 acres in size with a maximum depth of 28 feet, panfish and northern pike thrive in the lake.

Next, the trail slips between a pond and another wet meadow. The lake-pond terrain is part of the same geographical system that makes up the Chippewa Moraine State Recreation Area to the north. The region consists of irregularly-shaped lakes and ponds formed by glaciers at the end of the last ice age.

Upon reaching a trail junction, the loop portion of the route begins. Go left/west.

This takes you between Horseshoe (on the left/south) and Burnt Wagon (on the right/north) lakes. A ski shelter sits next to the trail on the Burnt Wagon Lake side.

Almost the entire trail is through a northern hardwood forest. In Wisconsin, such a forest typically consists of sugar maple, beech, basswood, white ash, and yellow birch. The trail makes for a colorful walk in autumn when the leaves change.

The loop next curves north along Burnt Wagon Lake's western shore. A 19-acre lake, Burnt Wagon has a depth of 17 feet.

On the lake's north side, the trail forks; going left/north takes you onto the North Loop. Continue straight/east, leaving the lake behind and passing a wet meadow on the left/north.

At the next junction, go right/southeast; the other way takes you onto another leg of the North Loop.

As the trail heads south, it passes a pond and then Silver Lake, both on the left/east. Though small at 2 acres, Silver Lake has a maximum depth of 16 feet so supports panfish, largemouth bass and northern pike.

The next trail junction is the stem you came in on. Continue straight/south back to the parking lot.

Friends of Hickory Ridge, a nonprofit, maintains the trails.

No fee is required to hike, but a donation box is at the

parking lot. Dogs are not allowed on the trails.

Other Hickory Ridge Recreation Area Trails

• **North Loop** – The 3.75-miles round trip trail mainly winds around Fishpole Lake. Park on the shoulder of the road west of Hay Meadow Trail road.

• **Tram Lake Loop** – To reach the trail, which winds around Tram Lake, head north on the western leg of the North Loop then take the first trail junction going right/east. Tram Lake Loop runs 2.2-miles. As with the North Loop, park on the road shoulder.

Lake Trail
Lake Wissota State Park

Day hikers can walk alongside ancient effigy mounds on a bluff overlooking a scenic blue lake at Lake Wissota State Park.

The Lake Trail runs 1.4 miles (2.8-miles round trip) with connectors running to other pathways. In all, 18 miles of hiking trails crisscross the park's 1000-plus acres of forests and prairieland.

To reach the state park and trailhead, from Chippewa Falls head north on Wis. Hwy. 178. Turn right/east onto County Road S. Immediately after the Chippewa River bridge, go right/east on County Road O. The park entrance is about two miles on the right. Park at the northernmost lot on park road.

At the lot's southwest corner, head to an overlook of Lake Wissota. The Chippewa River and several other waterways that merge in the general area feed the lake, which was formed in 1917 when a hydroelectric dam flooded the valley floor. The dam was built by the Wisconsin-Minnesota Light and Power Company, and an engineer on the project named the lake by combining part of "Wisconsin" (Wis) and of "Minnesota" (sota). The dam is still in operation and owned by Xcel Energy.

Today, the lake covers 6,024-acres and reaches a maximum depth of 72 feet. Walleyes and smallmouth bass dominate the lake, but fishermen also land largemouth bass, muskie, pike, panfish and even catfish.

From the overlook, follow the trail southeast as it parallels Lake Wissota. About 0.3 miles in, a connector leads back to the park road and the Red Pine Trail, so be careful to not make an accidental turn.

As the trail continues southward, it passes two long panther effigy mounds. These Native American ceremonial centers likely were used for centuries. The panther mound represents their builders' beliefs about the cosmos and society being divided into two parts – the upper world (sky) and the lower realm (Earth/water). A sign points out the mounds.

A little more than halfway to the trail's endpoint, the family campground appears on the left/northeast. Basswood, maples, oaks, and white pines cover the campground. A stairway heads down the bluff from the campground and trail to the lakeshore below.

The next trail intersection is the official Red Pine Trail, which heads left/north into an evergreen forest and tree plantation. Also called Norway pine, it's a common tree in Wisconsin and tends to grow in drier areas while being a favorite for tree plantations.

Within a few steps is another intersection with the connector heading left/west to the park road and the Jack Pine and the Fox trails.

Speaking of fox, common animals you'll see in the park - and you'll likely spot signs of some of them on the Lake Trail – include badger, beaver, fox, mink, otter, porcupine, weasel, and whitetail deer.

The Lake Trail ends at a swimming beach with a beach

house. A fishing pier is just beyond it.

After taking a swim to cool off, retrace your steps back up the trail to the parking lot.

Beaver Meadow Nature Trail
Lake Wissota State Park

An overlook of an abandoned beaver pond awaits day hikers on the Beaver Meadow Nature Trail in Lake Wissota State Park.

Many park visitors consider the 1.2-mile round trip to be among Lake Wissota's most scenic trails. Both summer and autumn mark great times to hike it, with each season offering its own play on the area's natural beauty.

To reach the trailhead, follow the same directions to the park as for the Lake Trail. Leave your vehicle in the lot off the park entry road just before the group campground.

The trail heads south from the lot across the park road and runs on a bluff top overlooking Lake Wissota. The man-made lake covers more than 6000 square acres.

After passing a small inlet of Lake Wissota, the stem comes to the loop. Go left/east on it.

Along the way, you'll pass through a pine forest and by a marsh. It's mostly shaded, however.

On the loop's east side, the pathway comes to a junction with Staghorn Trail. Stay on the main trail (or veer left).

You may want to bring a guidebook about Wisconsin plant life with you. The trail includes mushrooms, the rare ghost plant (aka as the Indian pipe), and ferns.

Coming to the loop's end, the trail reaches an overlook of the former beaver pond. Beavers build dams to keep predators at bay and to create ponds so that they have a ready supply of food during winter. Like human engineers, beavers begin their dam construction by diverting the stream's flow to lessen the amount of water pressure on their main dam when it's being built.

After taking in the views, cross the stream draining into the inlet, and follow the stem trail back to the parking lot.

As the trail heads past a bog and stream, it can be buggy. Hike the trail at midday when the heat will keep the insects at bay, and be sure to don and carry mosquito repellent with you in summer.

Other Lake Wissota State Park Trails

Eight major trails, many of which can be done in combination with another, ramble through the state park. Campgrounds and picnic grounds also are available. Among those trails, from northwest to southeast, are:

• **Old Abe State Trail link** –The paved railroad grade trail runs for 20 miles and connects the state park to Brunet Island State Park in Cornell or heads south across the Chippewa River into Chippewa Falls.

• **Plantation Trail** – A square route with the access trail runs about 1.4 miles through a red pines plantation. Hikers can reach the trail via the northwest corner of the Red Pine Trail.

• **Red Pine Trail** – The Nevada-shaped trail runs past a meadows and through a red pine forest for 1.5 miles (stem is 0.5 miles one-way, loop is 0.5 miles). Start from the lot off the main park road just beyond the campground.

• **Prairie Wildflower Nature Trail** – The self-guided 0.5-mile trail in the middle of the park offers an up-close view of tall grasses and a variety of other plants. In July, many flowers bloom, making for a beautiful walk.

• **Eagle Prairie Trail** – Shared by hikers and off-road bicyclists, the 0.5-mile (one-way) trail connects the Red Pine and Fox trails, and must be accessed via one of them.

• **Fox Trail** – The roughly square-shaped trail runs about 0.5-miles and is shared by hikers and off-road bicyclists. It can be reached either via Red Pine-Eagle Prairie tails or by heading up a segment of the Jack Pine Trail.

• **Jack Pine Trail** – The 0.75-mile loop is largely wooded. Reach it via the parking lot off the park entry road, just before the group campground.

• **Staghorn Trail** – Located in the park's southern section, the 2-mile loop intersects several other park trails. Access it via the parking lot off the park entry road, just before the group campground.

Irvine Park Loop
Irvine Park

Day hikers can enjoy a pleasant walk alongside a creek, through a tiny zoo, and past a cave at Irvine Park in Chippewa Falls.

Irvine Park heralds back to the day when cities set aside large swaths of land for multiple recreational purposes. It feels a lot like a miniature version of New York City's Central Park or Los Angeles' Griffith Park.

Multiple walking paths run through Irvine Park, but the popular wooded ski trail often listed as a hiking trail tends to be overgrown by late summer. A good alternative is a paved 1.1-mile loop through the park's southeast corner.

To reach the park, from downtown Chippewa Falls head north on Wis. Hwy. 124. Turn left/west onto Bridgewater Avenue. Go right/north onto Bear Den Drive and pull into the parking lot on the left/west.

From the parking lot, angle northeast past the restrooms. At Bear Den Drive, walk left/north along the sidewalk.

Formed in 1906 by Chippewa Falls resident William Irvine, the park now covers 318 acres. Irvine envisioned a park that preserved the area's natural history for all area residents to enjoy at no cost.

At Wolfe Drive, go left/northwest. A bridge crosses Duncan Creek and in short order enters the tiny zoo. Among the features are a duck pond, an exhibit including Bengal tigers, and a black bear exhibit.

As leaving the zoo, the trail follows Duncan Creek, offering various scenic views of it. Starting several miles north of the city near New Auburn, the stream in the park offers a number of small cascades before flowing into the Chippewa River.

Go right/southeast onto Irvine Park Drive and cross the creek. When the trail curves south alongside the creek, it becomes Bear Den Drive.

This portion of the hike focuses more on the area's natural setting. Duncan Creek runs on the trail's right/west side while sandstone walls line the left/east side.

Along the way is a small cave that can be entered. To the cave's south are a set of 60-foot high tiered rocks that can be scrambled up.

The rock is Mt. Simon sandstone, which formed about 495 million to 500 million years ago as Wisconsin rose from the sea. Most of the rock layers were created by sediment, as tidal currents reclaimed Wisconsin for the ocean.

Upon reaching the restrooms, angle southwest back to the parking lot.

Glen Loch Dam Trail
Irvine Park

A nearly 150-year-old dam and a century-old bridge over a deep, narrow ravine await day hikers on the Glen Loch Dam Trail in Chippewa Falls.

The 1.4-miles round trip trail sits in Irvine Park. It's not the official name of the trail that essentially follows two narrow park roads doubling as walking paths.

To reach the trailhead, from downtown Chippewa Falls head north on Wis. Hwy. 124. Turn left/west onto Bridgewater Avenue. Go right/north onto County Road Q/Wheaton Street then right/east onto County Road S. Head right/south onto Ermatinger Drive and upon entering Irvine Park, use the first parking lot on the left.

Walk south on Ermatinger Drive. The paved path is nicely shaded, and in autumn offers up great fall leaf displays.

Between the trees, you'll can catch views of Glen Loch. It covers 39 acres and was created by backing up Duncan Creek so the dam could power a sawmill managed by local businessman William Irvine. The Pure Ice Company cut frozen water from atop the lake beginning in 1935 and sold it as ice.

About 0.2 miles into the hike, the trail comes to the Rumble Bridge. The narrow, steel bridge – built in 1914 – crosses a deep ravine. Irvine paid for the bridge so parkgoers had access to the park's north side.

In 0.4 miles from the bridge, the walkway junctions with Irvine Park Drive. Turn left/southeast onto the road.

An overlook of the dam is in another 0.1 miles. Glen Loch Falls and an old saw mill structure sit at 900 feet elevation.

The Chippewa Lumber and Boom Company Sawmill built the dam in 1875 to serve what at the time was the world's largest sawmill within a single building. A mere four years later, Hector McRae erected a flour mill next to the dam. The mill could produce 100 barrels of flour a day. It was tore down in 1924.

The dam has survived three major floods. In 1959, it was modified. Today, it stretches 149 feet wide with a 37-foot drop.

When Wisconsin's logging days were over in the early 1900s, Irvine donated the lake and surrounding land to the city for a park.

Once taking in the view of the dam, retrace your steps back to the parking lot.

Elk Creek Fishery Trail
Elk Creek Fishery Area

A pleasant walk along a scenic trout stream awaits day hikers in southwestern Chippewa County.

The hike runs about a half-mile round trip at the Elk Creek Fishery Area near the border of Chippewa and Dunn counties.

To reach the trailhead, from Chippewa Falls head west on Wis. Hwy. 29. After about nine miles, go right/north on 40th Street then left/west on County Road X. A gravel road on the right/north leads to the parking area, which overlooks the creek.

From the parking lot, head west down a small hill to the creek. At the water's edge, turn right/north, following the meandering stream. Though there is no official trail here, the open meadow along its banks makes for an easy hike. Autumn is particular beautiful as the hardwoods and tag alder leaves change color.

In about 800 feet, you'll pass a small cascades.

In total, the fishery covers 330 acres and includes 3.3 miles of Elk Creek, a Class I trout stream. Such high quality streams are able to sustain a reproducing population of trout.

Brown trout dominates the main stream with brook trout present at its tributaries' confluences. You'll be able to see such a spot about 400 feet upstream from the cascades where a small stream flowing out of the surrounding farmlands joins with the main creek.

The confluence marks a good point to turn back. Upon reaching the spur heading up to the parking lot, however, instead continue walking downstream. Another small cascades appears about 150 feet from the spur.

Be sure to wear hiking boots as the grass and sandy ground along the streambanks can be wet.

Other Chippewa County Trails

• **Chapman Lake Trail** – A narrow footpath loops Chapman Lake with a couple of scenic white footbridges on the nearly 2-mile route in Stanley. Parking is available at Chapman Park off of West Eighth Avenue north of County Road O/ West Fourth Avenue.

• **Hay Meadow Horse trails** – The 22-mile equestrian trail system runs across glacial moraines through woodlands full of lakes, ponds and streams. An easy to access route is the Beaver Pond Trail, which runs east from a parking lot off of Hay Meadow Flowage Trail road north of 225th Avenue northeast of Bloomer.

• **Lafayette Trail** – A 1-mile trail runs through a woods next to the Town of Lafayette Town Hall and ball fields east of Chippewa Falls. Park at the town hall off of 197th Street.

• **Moon Ridge trails** – Located in the Chippewa County Forest northwest of Cornell, a number of trails (including the Ice Age National Scenic Trail) crisscross the maple, basswood and ash woodlands. Watch for trailheads off of Moon Ridge Trail road (aka 226th Street), south of County Road M, and park on the road's shoulder.

• **Riverview Reserve trails** – Two-miles of trails run in the eastern Chippewa Falls reserve near the Chippewa River and Lake Wissota. Park in the lot off of Beach Drive west of the 74th and 75th Avenue intersection.

• **Ruby County Forest trails** – A number of jeep trails run through the Town of Ruby County Forest northeast of Cornell and southwest of Lake Holcombe. One good trail is on the north side of 245th Avenue east of County Road G.

• **Tom Lawin Wildlife Area** – No designated trails run through the wildlife area and the Lawin Sedge Meadow State

Natural Area it surrounds, but there are a number of deer trails that traverse the grounds southeast of Jim Falls. Parking areas can be found along 127th Avenue (aka Wildlife Drive) and County Road K west and south of their intersection.

• **Wildflower Trail** – A short trail heads to an impressive spring wildflower display along the Chippewa River bottoms north of Jim Falls. Park in the gravel lot on the east side of Wis. Hwy. 178 south of 150th Avenue.

• **Witt Park Nature Walk** – A small trail winds through the Bloomer park that sits along the shore of Duncan Creek. The park is on Chippewa Road south of Main Street.

Eau Claire County

S itting in the county's northwest corner along the Chippewa River, Eau Claire is the Chippewa Valley's most populous city and the region's economic center. While a number of excellent trails, particularly the Chippewa River State Trail, are found there, the rest of the county also offers a number of excellent day hiking opportunities. A significant number of them run along or near the Eau Claire River, which flows from the county's eastern side into Eau Claire. The eastern terminus of the Buffalo River State Trail also is in the county. Trails in this section generally are listed from northwest to southeast.

Lakeshore Trail
Carson Park

Day hikers can walk a tranquil, wooded path that at one time was a hub of Wisconsin's bustling logging industry.

The Lakeshore Trail at Eau Claire's Carson Park runs about a mile one-way. A side trail of the Chippewa River State Trail, it's less of a wilderness route than an urban walking path.

To access the trail, from U.S. Hwy 12/Clairemont Avenue in Eau Claire, turn east onto Menomonie Street then left/north onto Carson Park Drive. Use the parking lot next to the baseball stadium. From there, cross Carson Park Drive and go southwest or northeast on the trail. Either direction, the path connects with the Chippewa River State Trail and could be walked in a loop.

The 134-acre park sits on a "peninsula" surrounded by an oxbow lake, Half Moon Lake, which once marked the course of the Chippewa River. Today, the river runs east and south of the lake.

Despite hugging Carson Park Drive, the path is quiet with the rustling of leaves in the wind far more common than passing vehicles. That wasn't the case during the last 1800s, though, when Half Moon Lake was a holding pond for logs awaiting their turn at the sawmill. In 1884, more than 989 million board feet of logs came down the Chippewa River to Eau Claire's sawmills. At the time, the Daniel Shaw Lumber Company owned what is now the park.

When the trees from up north were all felled, the lumber companies moved on, and for a while the peninsula sat empty and unused. Proposals included building a resort and a race-track there.

Then in 1914 the heirs of millionaire lumberman William Carson purchased the land and gave it to the city on condition that it be used as public park. The following year, the park was named for their father, the former president of Valley Lumber Company.

In the 1930s, a baseball stadium went up in the park. This was soon followed by the Paul Bunyan Logging Camp Museum, another museum for the county's history, and several other recreational facilities.

Chippewa River State Trail segment
City of Eau Claire

Day hikers can enjoy a pleasant urban hike along a river in the Chippewa Valley's largest city.

Though most of the Chippewa River State Trail runs through rural areas, its most used portion sits in the middle of Eau Claire. A 3.7-mile round trip segment of the trail links the Historic Water Street District to beautiful Phoenix Park.

People have used the route since at least 1882 when the Milwaukee Road set down a rail line on most of what is now the trail. The rail line was abandoned in 1980 and soon converted to a bicycling trail that also can be hiked. Like most former rail lines, the trail is fairly flat and wide (10 feet); much of it is also paved.

Start at the Chippewa River State Trail's 10th Avenue trailhead. From Menomonie/Water Street, drive south onto 10th Avenue; a small parking lot sits at the road's end southwest of Hobbs Memorial Ice Center. A short stem trail then connects the lot to the Chippewa River trail.

Once at the main trail, go right/north, heading through a quiet neighborhood. At Seventh Avenue, you must walk along the street. Turn right/east at Menomonie Street and then pick up the trail again at Sixth Avenue. The trail then passes through Historic Water Street District with the Chippewa River on the trail's right/south side.

The majority of the business buildings in the Water Street District were constructed in the early 1880s. At that time, the lumber industry was king in the Chippewa Valley with logs floating from the Northwoods down the Chippewa River to sawmills in Eau Claire.

Upon leaving the historic district, the trail passes through a small stretch of the University of Wisconsin-Eau Claire campus, specifically in front of the Haas Fine Arts Building. The university's music, theater arts, and arts programs, along with performance halls, are located there.

As the river curves north, so does the trail, crossing Water Street and running through Owen Park. Downtown Eau Claire sits on the opposite shoreline. At West Grand Avenue, a bridge crosses the Chippewa, linking the trail to downtown.

Next, the trail comes to the confluence of the Chippewa and Eau Claire rivers. North of the confluence, the trail swerves right/northeast and via a trestle bridge crosses the Chippewa and enters Phoenix Park.

A steel company sat on the site for decades, though you wouldn't guess that today. Several years after the manufacturer closed its doors, the city reclaimed the area as a green space, with the park opening in 2005. A Farmers' Market is held each Saturday at the park, making it an interesting urban hiking destination.

For day hikers, the park marks a good spot to turn back. The trail does continue east, though, following the Eau Claire River, with a spur crossing the waterway to the Fairway Trail, before swerving north at U.S. Hwy 53 on its way to Chippewa Falls.

Generally on the Chippewa River State Trail, passes are required for bicyclists, inline skaters, and horse riders but not for hiking or casual walking. Pets also are allowed but must be on a leash no longer than 8 feet long.

Alternate south route: Back at the parking lot, going left/south rather than right/north takes you to a junction with the Lakeshore Trail that circles to Carson Park, or you can continue south out of town to Caryville and on to Tarrant Park in Durand. The trail sticks to the Chippewa River shoreline the entire way.

• Also see entries for this trail in the Chippewa, Dunn and Pepin counties sections.

Eau Claire River Route
City of Eau Claire

Day hikers can walk across a unique S-shaped bridge on a short urban trail in downtown Eau Claire.

The 0.6-mile round trip Eau Claire River Route – often referred to on maps as a side trail of the Chippewa River State Trail – runs alongside and crosses its namesake. Its connections with the main Chippewa River State Trail allow for quick access to various city parks.

Park at the L.E. Phillips Memorial Library then cross South Dewey Street, heading east onto the paved trail. Breaks through the trees allow for views of the Eau Claire River, which in this stretch runs over a series of cascades.

The Eau Claire River is one of the Chippewa Rivers' major tributaries, flowing for 40 miles out of the east. Two nearby dams back it up into reservoirs.

With the elevation changes on the river, a variety of trees can be spotted along the way, making for a colorful autumn walk. Eau Claire is officially a Tree City USA, and a walk along this trail proves why.

In short order, the trail curves northeast and crosses the river on a trestle S bridge that originally served the railroad. The bridge offers great views of the river and of Banbury Place, which sits on the river's north side.

Now a complex of apartments, retail shops and offices, Banbury Place used to be the site of the Uniroyal tire plant that before closing its doors during the early 1990s was the city's largest employer. More than 1350 people worked at the 1.9 million-square-foot plant. The complex stretches a quarter-mile in length.

Upon reaching the Chippewa River State Trail on the river's north side, turn back. The Chippewa trail runs alongside busy Galloway Street and while pleasant for bicyclists, for hikers it's more akin to a sidewalk.

If you wish to continue, however, going left/west on the Chippewa trail takes you to beautiful Phoenix Park; you also can turn it into a loop by heading left/south at North Dewey Street and then head to the library. Going right/east on the trail offers access to Boyd Park and the Fairway Trail which leads to Archery Park; just past Banbury Place, turn right/south onto the trail that crosses that river and via a wood-chip path enters Boyd Park.

Putnam Trail State Natural Area trails
Putnam Park State Natural Area

Day hikers can enjoy a walk along two waterways through a wildlife-laden forest in the heart of western Wisconsin's largest metro area.

Several undesignated trails runs through the Putnam Park State Natural Area in Eau Claire, which boasts more than 70,000 residents. The University of Wisconsin–Eau Claire owns and maintains the 230-acre natural area.

Putnam Park actually consists of two sections, which the university campus splits. Both sections are narrow, curving strips along waterways.

The western section sits on the Chippewa River. To access it, from campus parking lot #4, follow the interpretive trail into the state natural area.

The much larger eastern section is largely centered on Little Niagara Creek. It can be reached by walking alongside Putnam Drive, which starts across from campus parking lot #14.

Both areas are heavily forested, with red and white pines dominating the higher ground while hackberry, paper and river birch, and red maple and silver maple thrive in the lower, wetter areas. Tamarack and white cedar also can be found in the eastern portion's wettest sections.

Day hikers will be impressed by the size of the trees, especially the red and white pine, which have largely been undisturbed for more than a century. Henry Cleveland Putnam donated the areas for the park to the city in 1909, wanting it set aside as a botanical laboratory because of the great variety of plants found there. Indeed, more than 400 species of plants have been documented.

With the diversity of plants and its size, the state natural area is a haven for an incredible range of animals for an urban area. At last count, 23 kinds of mammals – including beaver, white-tailed deer, and woodchucks – called the woods home. Six reptiles, including the prairie skink, also can be found there.

The state natural area is a great place for birdwatchers as well. About 100 bird species – such as eagles, hawks, wild turkeys, and woodpeckers – live there during summer.

One other species you're certain to find are college researchers documenting plants and animals. In 1957, the city transferred the acreage to the Wisconsin State College, which later became the university.

Ridgeline Trail
Lowes Creek County Park

Hikers can walk a forested trail overlooking a popular trout stream south of Eau Claire.

The Ridgeline Trail and the paths leading to it run 1.22-miles round trip at Lowes Creek County Park. About 18 miles of multi-purpose trails, frequented by hikers, runners and off-road bicyclists, can be found in the park, which hugs the creek's course.

To reach the trailhead, from Eau Claire, take Wis. Hwy. 93 south. At Golf Road, turn right/west. In 1.5 miles, turn left/south into S. Lowes Creek Road. The park entrance is in another 1.5 miles; go left/east onto Palomino Road. A parking lot, is at the road's end. An entrance fee is required.

From the parking lot's northwest side, take the wide trail heading straight north (Two other trails go east.). At the first trail junction, in 0.1 mile, turn right/east, crossing a footbridge over Lowes Creek.

Flowing out of the slope between the Chippewa and Buffalo river valleys to the south, Lowes Creek is a Class II trout stream that eventually makes it way into the Chippewa. Native brook trout can be found between the mouth of Clary Creek north to the Chippewa, but the stream is restocked with brown trout for sports fishing.

At the next trail junction, in 0.08 miles, go right/southeast. You'll parallel the creek for about 0.25 miles, passing the junction with the Onion Trail, and at last reach the Ridgeline Trail. Go right/south on the Ridgeline, which overlooks the creek about 50 feet below.

While much of the upland surrounding Lowe Creek consists of pine forests, the moist soil along the creek bed yields other trees, including birch, making this a nice trail to see harvest colors in autumn.

Follow the Ridgeline Trail for 0.18 miles until it intersects the Nemesis and Skull trails. This marks a good spot to turn back.

Tower Ridge Recreational Area trails
Tower Ridge Recreational Area

Day hikers can enjoy a pleasant walk through an oak forest on the Tower Ridge Recreation Area trails near Eau Claire.

About fifteen miles of cross-country ski trails run across both flat and hilly terrain at the rec area. The largest cross country ski complex in the Chippewa Valley, the trails can be hiked during other seasons.

To reach the rec area, from U.S. Hwy. 53 in Eau Claire, take County Road QQ east. In about five miles, turn left/north onto County Road L then take the next right/southeast into Tower Ridge. Entrance passes are required.

With the vast number of crisscrossing trails, getting lost is surprisingly easy in the small woodlands. You'll definitely want to bring a map. Fortunately, trail junctions are nicely numbered.

An easy 1-mile loop over flat ground starts at the parking lot's northeast corner. At junction 10, go right/east.

Follow this to junction 24; once there, go left/north. Continue straight/north at junction 23 then turn right/west at junction 22. Head straight/west at junctions 21, 19 and 20 on the loop's north side. After junction 20, the trail curves back to junction 10; from there, turn right/south and head into the parking lot.

The forest sits atop a plateau about a 100 feet above the Eau Claire River. A small knoll rises about a hundred feet above the plateau just northwest of the loop.

As cross-country ski trails, all of the rec area paths are wide and open, so you'll want to don a sunhat or sunscreen.

Big Falls Trail
Big Falls County Park

Day hikers can amble over the sands of a 550-million-year-old ocean and rock that is at least 1.85 billion years old at Big Falls County Park.

Though there's no designated trail, hikers easily can walk a half-mile along the river, over the sandbars and across the rock. The falls area is great spot for wading, sunbathing and picnicking.

To reach the park, from Eau Claire, take U.S. Hwy. 12 east. Turn left/north on N. Elco Road. At County Road SS (aka 9 Mile Creek Road), go right/east. This road runs out at County Road K (aka N. 130th Avenue); head left/north onto County K. Just before crossing the Eau Claire River, turn left/west onto Big Falls Forest Road. The sandy road heads straight to a parking lot.

From the lot, walk west toward the river. The sound of water rushing over the falls points the way.

The Eau Claire River turns sharply at this spot, spilling in two falls over outcroppings of gneiss. A 25-foot drop, millions of gallons per hour pour over the polished gneiss and boulders, forming a deep pool below the falls.

The sandrock on the river's shoreline belongs to the Mt. Simon formation. It formed about 550 million years ago when sediment settled at the bottom of a shallow ocean covering this part of the world.

The exposed base of the sandstone sits atop even older gneiss that formed many miles beneath the surface of the earth some 1.85 to 1.9 billion years ago. This rock at one time belonged to the Marshfield continent that existed in the Archean era. At that time, the area south of what is now the Wisconsin Northwoods marked the edge of the North American proto-continent with a great sea beyond. A chain of islands known as the Marshfield continent gradually collided with the North American proto-continent, ultimately expanding the land area of what is now Wisconsin.

Over time, the Eau Claire River has cut through all of the Mt. Simon sandstone here and is now rushing over and exposing even more of the erosion-resistant gneiss.

The 135-acre county park straddles both sides of the Eau Claire River, and there is a northern entrance on the opposite shoreline. When planning a trip here, be careful to not confuse it with Big Falls County Park near Kennan in Wisconsin's Price County, which is a couple of hours drive away.

Note: Another trail with the same name can be found at the nearby Beaver Creek Reserve.

Interior Loop
Beaver Creek Reserve

Day hikers can walk along a creek, through an oak savanna, and past a turtle pond on the Interior Loop at the Beaver Creek Reserve north of Fall Creek.

The 1.3-mile round trip runs through a small section of the 400 acres overseen by the Friends of Beaver Creek Reserve. A number of nature and conservation programs occur year-round at the reserve. It's also a research site, with recent programs focusing on American kestrels, saw-whet owls, bat calls, and stream monitoring.

To reach the reserve, from U.S. Hwy. 12 in Fall Creek, go north on County Road K north. The reserve is on the north side of the Eau Claire River. Park in the lot for the nature center on the right/south side of the road. From there, take a connector trail east to the trailhead.

The Interior Loop heads southeast to an observation deck overlooking Beaver Creek, a meandering trout stream that flows for eight miles into the Eau Claire River. The creek supports a self-sustaining trout population; about 60 percent of Wisconsin's streams require the addition of trout grown in hatcheries.

Staying on Beaver Creek's west side, the trail gradually veers west, heading through an oak savanna along the way. In Wisconsin, savannas are a meeting ground between the flat, drier prairies of the West and the hillier, wetter deciduous forests of the East. On the reserve's savanna, oak is the dominant tree.

Upon leaving the open area, the trail and the Boundary Loop merge. Go left/east on to the Boundary Loop to enjoy the swinging bridge and its views over the Eau Claire River, then head back onto the Interior Loop.

The south side of the Interior Loop parallels the river. A major tributary of the Chippewa River, the Eau Claire flows west into the city that bears its name.

Next, the trail curves north past a marsh. Grasses rather than trees dominate these wetlands, which serves as a home for a variety of aquatic birds. An observation deck allows hikers to pause and enjoy the scenery.

On the trail's north side, it passes a turtle pond. Turtles spend most of their lives in the water, and should you get close enough to see one, you'll notice they have webbed feet and long claws.

The trail then turns north and heads to the nature center. The center contains a number of exhibits about the reserve's many ecosystems. The parking lots are just north of the center.

Other Beaver Creek Reserve Trails

An variety of great trails await day hikers at the Beaver Creek Reserve. The county road splits the reserve in half, so its trails can be divided into two groups.

North trails

Six trails (listed here from southeast to northwest) are located north of County Road K:

• **Youth Camp Trail** – The 0.6-miles one-way trail leaves from the Citizen Science Center/Wildlands School and passes the main lodge to the Exercise Loop. Park at the science center.

• **Naturalist Loop** – The 0.2-mile loop runs part of the way alongside Deinhammer Creek. Access it via the Youth Camp Trail.

• **Exercise Loop** – The 0.9-miles trail sits between Cedar Lodge and the Eau Claire River. Park in the lot for the observatory and walk west past the lodge.

• **Pine Loop** – Deinhammer Creek runs along two sides of the 0.85-mile loop. The quickest way to reach it is via the Youth Camp Trail then taking the connector trail across the creek.

• **Oak Loop** – The reserve's longest trail on the north side at 1.2 miles, the quickest way to reach it is via the Pine Loop. A connector trail from the Exercise Loop also links to it.

• **Big Falls Trail** – A 0.8-mile trail heads from the northwest corner of the Oak Loop along the Eau Claire River.

South trails

Located south of County Road K, park at the Nature Center for all trails (listed here from northeast to the southwest):

• **Savannah Loop** – A 0.6-mile trail runs past a creek, through an oak savanna, and by the turtle pond.

• **River Loop** – The 1.3-mile loop offers the longest stretch of trail along the creek and river at the reserve.

• **Boundary Loop** – The reserve's longest trail at 2.5 miles, it includes several footbridges, a picnic area, and an observation deck for a marsh.

Channey Forest Road
South Fork Barrens State Natural Area

Day hikers stand a good chance of spotting the rare and beautiful Karner blue butterfly in the South Fork Barrens State Natural Area.

The 1.4-mile round trip hike Channey Forest Road heads through a Jack pine-oak barrens. It's the perfect habitat for the Karner, which is rapidly disappearing in the Untied States.

To reach the state natural area, from Stanley, drive south on County Road H. Turn right/west onto E. Channey Forest Road. In a half-mile, the road comes to the border of the state natural area. At the first jeep trail heading north, park on the road shoulder.

While there are a lot of spur trails running off of E. Channey Forest Road, most of them quickly enter private property. Instead, walk alongside the shoulder of the gravel forest road. While this can be dusty in summer, the flat road is little traveled and ensures you stay on public land.

On either side of the road, you'll see a lot of Jack pine with bur oak, some Hill's oak and red pine, and blueberry and American hazelnut in the understory. There's also plenty of prairie grasses and forbs in the openings.

Among them is wild lupine, a favorite food plant of the Karner. Thanks to destruction of habitats where wild lupine thrives, the Karner's range is shrinking. At one time, it could be found from Minnesota to Maine, but today it's limited from Wisconsin to New York, and then in only very specific locales.

Extremely small – an adult Karner is only the width a nickel with an inch-long wingspan – the male's top side is a striking deep blue. The female's top side is a bit lighter blue with brown mixed in. Both genders' undersides consist of a curve of orange crescents near the wing edges.

As the Karner's pale green caterpillar feeds on lupines, the state uses prescribed burns to prevent woody plants from encroaching on the small sandy barrens where the flower grows.

When the road begins turning straight north in about 0.7 miles from where you parked, head back.

Augusta Wildlife Area Trail
Augusta Wildlife Area

Day hikers can explore an region being restored to its pre-settlement habitat on the Augusta Wildlife Area Trail.

The 1.2-miles round trip jeep trail sits in the 2,503-acre Augusta Wildlife Area between Augusta and Lake Eau Claire. The trail is one of many undesignated paths that cut through the state-run public land.

To reach the trailhead, from Augusta head north on County Road G. After Solie Road, take the first unnamed dirt road going right/east. This heads into the wildlife area. Park at the road's end.

From there, the trail heads straight southeast into a woods. Before the 1930s, white, black and bur oaks, with a few white and red pines, dominated the southern part of the wildlife area while Jack pine, scrub oak, and oak barrens covered the northern half. Most of it was cut down while wildfire burned the rest.

The trail next curves south and passes a pond on the left/east with wetlands just beyond the woodline. Melting glaciers formed those peat and marshlands about 10,000 years ago. At the time of the timber harvest, the marshlands were drained away, resulting in major habitat loss for ducks and geese.

Once past the pond, the trail curves west and enters an open area.

Beginning in the early 1940s, the state purchased land here in an effort to restore the wetlands. Three flowages were added over nine years while potholes and ditches were constructed.

Today, the area is populated with blue-winged teal, mallards and wood duck. Muskrats, beaver, ruffed grouse, and whitetail deer also call the wildlife area home.

Where the grassland gives way to field, turn back and retrace your steps to where you parked.

Some maps also refer to the public facility as the Augusta State Wildlife Area.

Coon Fork Lake Trail
Coon Fork County Park

Day hikers can enjoy a wooded trail along a scenic lake in Coon Fork County Park.

The 2.6-miles round trip Coon Fork Lake Trail hugs the shoreline of picturesque Coon Fork Lake in southeastern Eau Claire County. A number of mountain bike trails and more than three miles of ski trails also can be found in the park.

To reach the trail, from Augusta, take U.S. Hwy 12 south. Turn left/northeast onto County Road CF. After crossing Coon Fork Creek, go left/north onto Horse Creek Road. The dirt lot is immediately on the left/west. Carefully cross County CF and pick up the hiking trail as it heads south.

From there, the trail passes the east side of the dike that backs up Coon Creek to form Coon Fork Lake. Built in 1963, the dam is 20 feet high. The county park was created the year after the dam went into operation.

Beyond the dam, the trail then slips between the lake and Campground D and passes a boat landing. The looping campground is the newest one at the park.

The wooded trail parallels the lake's edge the rest of the way, offering several tree-framed vistas. Coon Fork Lake covers 62 acres. Musky, largemouth bass and panfish all are plentiful in the lake. At the southeast side of the lake, the trail crosses a small beach.

Songbirds are common on the trail. You're also likely see whitetail deer or at least signs of them such as their prints. Raccoons and even porcupines also have been spotted.

When the trail curves east, the lake significantly narrows and becomes Black Creek. Upon reaching the mountain bike trail at junction 28, the hiking trail ends, marking a good spot to turn back.

If a dog owner, the county park trail is a good spot. Pets are allowed here on leashes of up to eight feet.

Buffalo River State Trail segment

Day hikers can enjoy a pastoral walk past farm fields and through country woods on the Buffalo River State Trail.

The trail runs for 36.4 miles through the Buffalo River Valley between Mondovi and Fairchild while passing three other farm towns. Most of the way, the trail parallels either the Buffalo River or one of its forks. An easy to reach and rustic segment to walk heads 4.8-miles round trip from Fairchild to the North Fork Buffalo River.

To reach that trailhead in Fairchild, at Eau Claire County's southeastern corner, from U.S. Hwy. 12 go northeast onto

County Road YY/North Street. After crossing Town Line Road, turn left/north into the Buffalo River State Trail parking lot. An access trail goes from the lot north to the main route.

Once there, turn left/southwest onto the trail (Taking the trail the other direction heads into downtown Fairchild.). Built on a former railroad grade, the trail here and throughout its course is fairly flat with a surface of railroad ballast and limestone screenings.

In about 0.1 miles, the trail crosses busy Hwy. 12. Be sure to look both ways and hold hands of any children with you.

From there, the trail is nicely lined with hardwood trees on both sides, making for a pleasant colorful walk in autumn. The trail is wide, though, so you'll need a sunhat or sunscreen.

Through breaks in the trees, you'll be able to spot a variety of farm fields on either side of the tracks. This is classic Wisconsin dairy country you're heading through.

About 0.5 miles from trailhead, the trail crosses McGower Road. In doing so, you are now in Jackson County. At 0.9 miles, the trail intersects Arndt Road.

The farmland gives way to heavier woodlands at about 1.85 miles, when the trail recrosses McGower Road. Tree plantations can be seen on the trail's north side for part of this segment.

At 2.4 miles, the trail reaches North Fork Buffalo River, a good turnback point. The river and its forks were named by early French explorers for the bison than once roamed this area; they called it the Riviere de Beeufs. The North Fork joins the main Buffalo River upstream. The Buffalo in turn flows into the Mississippi River at Alma; it's the next tributary to feed the southbound Mississippi after the Chippewa River.

Bicycles, horses, ATVs and UTVs also use the trail spring

through autumn; during winter, it becomes a snowmobile trail. Be aware that sometimes maps refer to the route as the Beef River Recreational Vehicle Trail or as the Buffalo River State Park Trail.

Other trailheads (heading east to west) for the trail include:

• **Osseo** – On non-school days, park at the school's athletics fields the at northern end of Rose Lane. Follow the lane north onto an access trail for the Buffalo River State Trail.

• **Strum** – Park downtown on County Road D/Fifth Avenue South; the trail is between Birch and Maple streets.

• **Eleva** – Park on Third Street South and walk south; the trail is just past Goddard Street.

• **Mondovi** – Parking is available at the southern end of Marten Street.

Other Eau Claire County Trails

• **Altoona Trail** – Several segments of a plan to construct a 15-mile loop of bicycle and walking trails are completed in Altoona and neighboring Eau Claire. Currently, the segments link Lake Altoona County Park to Eau Claire's Phoenix and Carson parks. Vehicle lots are available at all three parks.

• **City Wells Area Trail** – A 3-mile looping cross-country ski trail in Eau Claire's City Wells area can be day hiked the other seasons. Start the loop off of Riverview Drive near the southeast corner of Riverfront Park.

• **Fairfax Park walking paths** – About 1.17 miles of walking paths (turned cross-country ski trail in winter) run around two ponds and through a small woods at Eau Claire's Fairfax Park. Leave your vehicle in the parking lot for the outdoor pool then cross Fairfax Park Drive for the trailhead in the wooded area.

• **Fairway Trail** – The 1.4-miles round trip in Eau Claire links Boyd and Archery parks, running between Fairway

Street (on its south) and the Eau Claire River (on its north).

• **Lake Eau Claire County Park** – A 0.4-mile round trip jeep trail runs through a pine barrens in the park located north of Augusta on man-made Lake Eau Claire. Park off the shoulder of County Road SD immediately west of Sd Lane.

• **Paul Bunyan Logging Camp Museum walking trail** – An informal 0.1-mile trail winds from the museum's main building through several smaller ones that gives a good understanding of what life was like in a Northwoods logging camp of the late 1800s. Parking is available at the museum in Eau Claire's Carson Park.

• **Pinehurst Park Trails** – Nearly a mile of hilly trails (used as a cross-country ski trails in winter) sit in the park on Eau Claire's north side. Leave your vehicle in the parking lot off Delbert Road between Eastlawn and Oakland streets.

• **Sherman Creek Park walking paths** – Footpaths run alongside and cross Sherman Creek in the 30-acre wooded park located just west of Eau Claire in Union Township. Access the trail off of West Vine Street between Deblene and Redwood lanes.

Dunn County

Most of Dunn County consists of splendid farmland, though the Red Cedar River corridor running south from through Menomonie to the Chippewa River offers outdoor recreational opportunities. The bulk of the county's trails are located in or near the city of Menomonie – whose name is derived from the local Native American word for "wild rice people" – which is centered on Lake Menomin, a former marshy area along the now dammed Red Cedar. Trails in this section generally are listed northeast to southwest.

Tower Nature Trail
Hoffman Hills State Recreation Area

Day hikers can see a dozen major trees that dominate Wisconsin forests while heading to a 60-foot observation tower in Hoffman Hills State Recreation Area.

The roughly two-mile Tower Nature Trail sports a lot of steep ups and downs, so preschoolers and young elementary children may have trouble making it all the way without being carried. It's a good workout for moderately fit adults, but the payoff – in views and better health – is worth the effort.

To reach the trail, from Exit 45 on Interstate 94 east of Menomonie, take County Road B north. Turn right/east onto 650th Avenue, which eventually becomes County Road E. Follow County Road E/730th Street as it goes north. The highway zigzags to the park entrance, which is a little more than a mile north of 690th Avenue. Follow the park entrance road to the main parking lot.

Look for the trailhead at the center of the parking lot's east side. The trail is fairly smooth and wide, usually consisting of mowed grass, though some of the slopes are sandy.

It's mostly shaded.

From the parking lot, the trail heads up then downhill though a stand of birch and maple with an understory of ferns. During autumn, the yellow birch and red maple leaves make a splendid display.

The two trees dominating this section of the trail played an important role in Wisconsin history. Native Americans from this area used birch bark to make canoes, wigwams, baskets and cups. The maple was used by pioneers for furniture and today is a major source of syrup.

As the trail heads downhill, it enters a large stand of red pines. Also known as Norway pines, the tree is named for a town in Maine, not the country, as it's native only to North America.

At 0.4 miles, the trail reaches the Whispering Pines Group Camp, an open area with a shelter, water pump, pit toilet, and fire pit. Head north at the four-corner trail junction in the camp.

The trail continues uphill for another 0.4 miles, with the trail transitioning from red pines to maples. At the next trail junction, go right/east then in about 500 feet go left/north. Watch for blue jays and chipmunks and in the trail sand the tracks of white-tailed deer.

White pines can be found amid the maples in this section of the trail. During the 1800s, white pines were extensively logged off the Wisconsin landscape. What lumberjacks didn't finish, modern industrialization may complete; white pines are extremely sensitive to air pollution and rapidly disappearing.

Ridgelines can be followed along two side trails at two different spots in this area. Each adds about 0.45 miles to the hike, though, as they loop off and back onto the main trail.

As the Tower Nature Trail closes on the highest elevation in Hoffman Hills and the surrounding landscape, red oaks begin to dominate. Watch for the aptly named red squirrel, which likes red oaks, and if you're hiking during early autumn, listen for the *plink* of falling acorns as they hit the ground.

The red oaks soon give way to white oaks, which brings you to the hill's crest. At the top is the 60-foot Greg Schubert Memorial Tower, erected during the 1980s by the U.S. Army Reserve.

From the observation tower's top platform, you can see about six miles on a clear day. A pretty quilt of farm fields and woodlands stretch below the hill in all directions.

Continuing west from the tower, the trail is largely downhill. Look for sumac, with its red fruit in fall, in the understory.

At the next trail junction, go right/west. You'll loop around the hillside as losing elevation, passing quaking aspen and then hawthorn and dogwood along the way. Continue straight through the next junction. The route eventually re-enters the stand of red pines that stretches a fifth of a mile to the group camp area.

Turn right/west at the next trail junction. You'll skirt a meadow to your left and a wooded area sporting white ash trees on the right. An extremely hard wood, white ash is used to make baseball bats.

In about 1000 feet, turn left/south; if you go straight, you'll end up in the overflow parking lot. The trail's last 1000 feet pass through a birch stand. To the right between the thin trees you can spot a prairie area across the park road.

At last the trail ends in an open grassy area with picnic tables, water pump and restrooms. The main parking lot is south of the open area.

Be forewarned that a number of trails branch off the main route, so keep an eye on trail markers and posted maps to stay on course. Should you accidentally take the wrong turn, the trail typically will loop back, but you'll easily add a half-mile or more to your walk.

These adjoining trails do provide an excellent opportunity to teach older children about map reading. They can follow a printed map of the recreation area, and when you see a trail marker, ask them where you are on the map then compare it to the signage, which nicely includes a "you are here" star.

Catherine Hoffman Hartl Memorial Wetland Trail
Hoffman Hills State Recreation Area

Day hikers can enjoy a walk through a restored prairie and around two tranquil ponds on the Catherine Hoffman Hartl Memorial Wetland Trail.

The 0.76-mile trail at Hoffman Hills State Recreation Area is a few miles northeast of Menomonie. To reach the trail, follow the same directions as for the Tower Nature Trail.

Walk north from the parking lot into the grassy picnic area, looking for the sign pointing toward the trail. Cross the park road, and you've reached the trailhead. The trails are wide and mowed with a few interpretive signs along the way.

The trail skirts a restored prairie dominated by big bluestem grass. Big bluestem roots can grow up to 12 feet underground, and the stem itself can grow up to 8 feet high. In September, the yellow stems of this field usually reach about five feet high, impressive to child and adult alike.

As late as the 1800s, such prairies were common in southern Wisconsin before pioneers plowed them under into farm fields. Patches of such prairie existed as far north as Dunn County with bison and elk inhabiting them.

The trail next edges a wooded hillside dominated by birch then curves north through the prairie. At 0.17 miles, a short trail leads to a rocky knoll with a bench overlooking the bluestem.

Continuing north, the trail gradually becomes more wooded as passing quaking aspen. Keep an eye out here for some of the recreation area's wildlife, including white-tailed deer, red-tailed hawk and mallard ducks – and if you're lucky, even a great blue heron. You're certain to hear a number of insects and songbirds as well. Several birdhouses sit just off the trail.

At 0.3 miles, the trail heads under a set of majestic weeping willows. At the trail junction immediately after the willows, go left/west.

The trail then runs through an idyllic glade on the south side of a pond. Curve clockwise around the pond, and on its northwest side at the next junction turn left/west.

As the trail cuts through wetlands, watch for a number of plants native to marshes in this part of Wisconsin. Among them are the arrowleaf violet, brittle gentian, great blue lobelia, marsh marigold, sweet Joe-Pye weed, and white turtlehead.

The trail then loops around a second, larger and prettier pond. Go clockwise through the glade. On the north side is a stem trail leading to a bench at the pond's shoreline.

Follow the trail back through the wetlands to the first pond. This time, however, walk along the pond's north side.

At the next junction, day hikers with a little extra energy can turn left/north onto a connecting trail for a couple of loops (the western loop is 0.6 and the eastern loop 0.68 miles) through the northern portion of the restored prairie area. These loops are a bit less maintained, however, so you probably won't want to walk them unless wearing jeans.

If not doing those extra loops, return to your vehicle by going right/south and following the trail past the east side of the pond then back under the willows and through the prairie to the parking lot.

Elk Mound Swamp trails
Red Cedar Waterfowl Production Area and Muddy Creek Wildlife Area

A couple of protected areas in the Elk Mound Swamp offer great bushwhacking country.

The Red Cedar Waterfowl Production Area and the Muddy Creek Wildlife Area are both conveniently located near the freeway in west-central Dunn County. Though there are no designated paths, some deer and jeep trails do cut across both areas.

Red Cedar Waterfowl Production Area

From Menomonie, take Interstate 94 east then turn onto County Road B south. Go left/east onto 610th Avenue; turn right/south onto 730th Avenue. A parking lot is on the road's left/east side. Cross the road and head west into the production area.

A U.S. Fish & Wildlife Service property, the area provides nesting and feeding grounds for waterfowl. Migratory birds – including songbirds – often can be spotted here in spring and fall.

Though only 336.1 acres in size, the production area is a vital zone for waterfowl, as Wisconsin has lost about 2 million hectares of wetland since gaining statehood in 1848. The Red Cedar WPA adjoins the Strehlau Waterfowl Production Area to the north.

Muddy Creek Wildlife Area

From Interstate 94, at Exit 52 take U.S. Hwy. 12/Wis. Hwy. 29 west. Watch for the parking area on the highway's right/north side. A gated jeep trail leads from the parking loop's northwest corner into a woods that hugs Muddy Creek's banks.

Most of the state wildlife area's 4100 acres consists of

marshy lowlands, known locally as the Elk Mound Swamp. But amid the wetlands are islands of prairie and woodlands, the latter mainly consisting of aspen, oaks and white pine. Farm fields along the wildlife area's edges have been converted to tallgrass prairie.

For ecologists, though, the wetlands are what prove most interesting. As a transition zone, the area is one of the few spots in Wisconsin where plant species from both northern and southern sedge meadows can be found.

Bushwhacking tips

While you'll want to stick to deer trails or vehicle tracks, as much as possible when visiting these two areas, that won't always be possible. Don't cut grass with a machete, however, and tread lightly no matter where you walk.

Be aware that whether you stay on a trail or bushwhack, the ground can be soft and muddy. Because of this, hiking boots definitely are needed during any visit.

You'll also want to wear pants as the grass often will be high and wet. Avoid denim jeans and cotton shirts, which when wet are difficult to dry out, though a cotton/poly combo usually is okay.

Tall grasses are ideal spots for ticks, but they can be kept off you by wearing long-sleeved shirts and tying each pants leg bottom tight over your boots. Always check your body afterward for any hitchhiking critters.

Mound Hill Park Castle Trail
Mound Hill Park

Day hikers can visit what looks like the ruins of a Medieval castle in Elk Mound.

A very brief walk – at most 0.2 miles-round trip – the Mound Hill Park Castle – sits atop a tall hill surrounded by an expansive woods. The castle, located at Mound Hill Park, closes when snow and ice cover the steep, narrow road leading to it.

To reach the trail, from downtown Elk Mound, head north on County Road H/North Holly Avenue. Go right/east onto Elk Mound Hill Road, taking the one-and-a-half lane to the top of hill. A looping parking lot is at the road's end.

From the lot, walk south to a staircase that leads up to the tower. Made of gray stone, it looks more like a turret of a long-since destroyed castle. It has three floors with its windows offering great views of the village below and the surrounding countryside.

The mound certainly is a good place to build a tower. At 1220 feet elevation, Native Americans once used the hilltop to spot elk and buffalo herds on the plains below.

Because the mound is among the highest points on the horizon, in 1926 a contractor who constructed U.S. Hwy. 12 to the south erected a flagpole on the hilltop. Then in 1934, a tree planted atop the mound was dedicated as a memorial to county postal workers who'd passed away, with soil from each of their routes placed around the tree.

In 1937, the Works Progress Administration and Dunn County constructed the 25-foot high observation tower. Its stones come from a quarry in nearby Downsville while other materials were culled from a livery stable in Elk Mound.

The county closed the park in 1987, citing issues with the road leading up the mound. The castle rose like a phoenix, though – for the next six years, Elk Mound High School students worked to restore the park as part of a community service project. The site reopened as a village park in 1994 with a new flagpole and lighting later added.

Menomin Park Loop
Menomin Park

A pleasant walk alongside a lake and through restored

prairie awaits day hikers on the Menomin Park Loop.

About 12 miles of mountain biking trails and several walking paths head through the county-owned Menomin Park, which is largely undeveloped and used to mostly be farmland.

A great way to see the highlights of the 151.6-acre park is a 1.9-miles lollipop trail.

To reach the trailhead, from Wis. Hwy. 29 in eastern Menomonie, take Red Cedar Drive north. After the street becomes Domain Drive, turn onto the dirt road heading left/ north side. A parking lot is at the road's end.

From the lot, the trail meanders north through a restored prairie land. At the first trail junction, go left/east, beginning the loop.

The trail then curves northwest along Lake Menomin's shoreline. The quarter of a mile is forested on one side.

At 1009 acres, Lake Menomin is a man-made reservoir caused by the damming of the Red Cedar River. The lake reaches a maximum depth of 34 feet and sports largemouth and smallmouth bass, northern pike, panfish, and walleye.

As the trail curls east away from the lake, it crosses a small stream and turns south, skirting a small wetlands with prairie on the other side. The prairie grasses can get quite tall here in summer.

At the next trail junction, turn left/east. There's a woods on one side and prairie on the other.

Take the next trail heading right/south. This runs through a forested area.

At the next trail junction, go left/east and then at the one after that, turn right/south. This places hikers back on the stem trail leading to the parking lot.

Great news for dog owners: Fido is allowed at the park.

Be aware that various literature sometimes refers to the area as 3M Park or as Lake Menomin Park.

Lions Club Game Park Nature Trail
Lions Club Game Park/Wakanda Park

Day hikers can seek buffalo, elk, deer and waterfowl up close on the Lions Club Game Park Nature Trail in north Menomonie.

The 0.5-mile loop at the Lions Club Game Park essentially circles a pond with animal enclosures that are always on at least one side of the trail. There's no fee to enter.

To reach the trailhead, from U.S. Hwy. 12/N. Broadway Street in Menomonie, go east on Pine Avenue. Upon reaching Wakanda Park, turn left/north onto Game Park Road. A parking lot is at the road's end.

Animal pens can be found on the parking lot's east side. The buffalo enclosure is on the north side.

Upon reaching the buffalo, head right/east on the trail between the fences. The route here cuts between two ponds.

The buffalo eat about 600 bales of hay a year while the elk scarf down 12 large round bales. If the animals approach you, don't be afraid – they're just expecting a little something to eat, and feeding them is entirely okay here. All of them enjoy leftover garden greens, especially corn, and the elk particularly like green leaves from deciduous trees.

At the next trail junction, turn right/southeast. You can go the opposite direction, but that heads toward the freeway so can be noisy.

The freeway, though, is the whole reason the park came to be. During the 1950s when Interstate 94 was being built here, community leaders thought adding elk that could be seen from the freeway would be a good way to bring people to town. It worked, and today people still can spy some of the animals, usually the buffalo, as zooming down the freeway.

When the trail reaches the next junction, turn right/west. The dirt road going left/east leads to a street. As the trail heads along the south side of pond, look for the ducks, geese and pheasants that have staked out a claim in the wetlands and wooded areas.

Once the trail reaches Game Park Road, turn right/north, and walk along the fenced side back to the parking lot. A couple of animal enclosures are located along this leg of the trail.

Red Cedar State Trail segment

Bald eagles, churning rapids, and a weeping wall await day hikers on a segment of the Red Cedar State Trail in Menomonie.

Running 14.5 miles alongside the Red Cedar River, the trail is too long to enjoy via a day hike. But with its many access points, the trail can be done in segments. Among the most scenic of them is the 1.6-mile (3.2-miles round trip) section from Riverside Park to the Devil's Punchbowl.

To reach the trailhead, from downtown Menomonie take Wis. Hwy. 29 west. Upon crossing the Red Cedar River bridge, turn at the second left (or south) into Riverside Park. A parking lot sits next to an old train depot turned visitor center, with the trail leaving from the lot's south end.

The trail runs atop a reclaimed railroad bed. Because of that, it's wide, fairly level, and hugs the river almost the entire way.

Heading south from the parking lot, the trail first passes the foundation of what once was a wooden building housing the locomotive and tender that made a daily run between here and Durand. A spur of the Old Milwaukee Road, the line was abandoned in 1973. Eight years later, it was reclaimed as a bicycle and hiking path.

Next the trail crosses Gilbert Creek, which flows into the Red Cedar. Remains of the old steel girder railroad bridge now hold up the footbridge.

From the creek, several breaks in the treeline offer framed views of the Red Cedar. The river flows 85 miles from Lake Chetac in Washburn County through the cities of Rice Lake and Menomonie on its way south to the Chippewa River.

Maples, pines, aspen, birch and oak can be found alongside the trail. Ferns often fill the understory of the embankment on the trail's west side.

A number of animals make their home in the river valley. Most dramatically on this section of the trail, bald eagles usually can be seen atop trees spying the waterway for a meal, while sandhill cranes sometimes make their way up from a wetlands further south on the river. Squirrels and chipmunks also can be spotted.

Much of the next several hundred yards offers a tranquil walk with only the sound of songbirds and rustle of leaves.

Close to a mile into the walk, the river bends again, and the sound and sight of riffles dominates. Riffles form when a shallow waterway curves over a coarse streambed. The result is a mini-rapids. Past the next footbridge is a bench for hikers to rest and enjoy the riffles.

Continuing south, the trail next passes a weeping wall, or layers of sandstone from which springs drip water down the rock face. Plants cling to the ledges where they can catch the water, making for a hanging gardens. The wall stretches for a couple of hundred feet.

At the 1.6 mile mark, you'll cross a stream flowing out of the famous Devil's Punchbowl. Unfortunately, there's no path from the Red Cedar into the Punchbowl gorge other than walking through the creek itself.

A picnic table sits at that stream's entry into the Red Cedar. This marks a good spot for a quick rest and to turn back.

On the return, you'll catch new views of the river and also

of the distant University of Wisconsin-Stout clock tower, an iconic symbol of Menomonie.

Other segments

Other trailheads (heading north to south) for the Red Cedar State Trail include:

• **Irvington** – Access the trail from the parking lot off of Paradise Valley Road immediately north of County Road D/440th Avenue in Irvington. The trail runs 2.7 miles north to Menomonie's Riverside Park and 4.3 miles south to Downsville.

• **Downsville** – Parking is in Downsville off of County Road C east of Wis. Hwy. 25. The trail can be taken north under the bridge and over the river to Irvington or 6.7 miles south to the Dunnville Bottoms.

• **Dunnville Bottoms** – The trail crosses County Road Y at the Dunnville Road intersection. A parking lot is available directly across the river; you'll have to walk along the county road bridge to the trail access. It heads north to Downsville and 0.9 miles south to the Chippewa River State Trail.

• Also see the entry for this trail in the Pepin County section.

Devil's Punchbowl Trail

Devil's Punchbowl Scientific Study Area

Intrepid souls can explore an allegedly haunted glen west of Menomonie.

A 0.25-mile round trip trail at the Devil's Punchbowl Scientific Study Area takes day hikers to a waterfall and a gorge carved out of sandstone. Be sure to also keep an eye out for strange balls of light that many claim maneuver about the surrounding woods.

To reach the trail, from Menomonie head west on Wis. Hwy. 29. Turn left/south onto County Road P then left/

southeast onto 410th Street. Look for the parking lot on the left/east side of the road between 490th and 450th Avenue.

The hike begins with a descent from the parking lot down a stairs to the waterfall's lip, which is made of hard sandstone. By midsummer, the stream is a mere trickle; waterflow is fairly good during the spring snowmelt, though. The water drops into the Punchbowl, a gorge through which the intermittent stream makes it way to the Red Cedar River.

Next, return to the parking lot and follow the trail heading southeast. This cuts along the edge of a meadow then enters a woodlands. Once there, a wooden stairs winds to the bottom of the gorge, which is about 60 feet deep.

The gorge is strikingly beautiful, a fern-covered glen with a light sheen of moss growing over the rock walls, as water from the falls fans out across small rocks in the streambed.

The gorge walls are compressed layers of sediment – aka sandstone – which settled at the bottom of warm tropical sea that covered this region around 500 million years ago.

Flooding from glacial meltwater carved out the soft sandstone around 10,000 years ago. Springs now drip water out of the recessed portions of the walls, which in winter results in otherwordly ice formations.

Beyond the intriguing geology may be something even more fantastic – strange orbs of light that some have reported at the site. These orbs apparently are able to change their size, shape and color, as they shift between trees. Other visitors at night have claimed to hear disembodied voices and strange noises.

Among the rarer stories is that of meeting small, gnome-like people. The pointy-eared creatures (replete with pointed hat) are about three- to four-feet tall.

The creek can be followed east to the river where it intersects with the Red Cedar Trail. By late June, though, the creek's shores beyond the glen usually are overgrown and generally impassable – unless you're an orb of light, of course.

Bjornson Education-Recreation Center Loop
Bjornson Education-Recreation Center

Day hikers can enjoy a pleasant walk through woodlands and past a small, spring-fed creek on a looping trail at the Bjornson Education-Recreation Center south of Knapp.

The 1.7-mile loop actually is a set of interconnecting trails at the 443-acre school forest owned by the School District of the Menomonie Area. A plethora of walking paths and logging trails, which double as cross country ski routes in winter, run through the recreation center.

Any day in summer and weekends during late spring and early autumn marks a good time to visit. Weekdays during the school year can be crowded and noisy as school kids may be on the site for classwork.

To reach the recreation center, from Interstate 94 west of Menomonie, take Exit 32 north on County Road Q. Turn right/east onto 700th Avenue then right/southwest onto 160th Avenue. As 160th Avenue curves sharply south, turn right/southwest onto the recreational center's main entrance road. Park off the entrance road in front of the gate. Do not drive past the gate, as you may get locked in.

Walk the entrance road into the center, passing a man-made pond along the way. During the 1970s, beavers constructed a natural pond upstream, but their overeagerness caused a great amount of flooding, forcing their removal; to compensate for the lost educational opportunity, the pond and wetlands alongside the entrance road were developed.

In about 0.4 miles, you'll reach the main group area, which includes a shelter, picnic tables, and pit toilets. On the group area's north side, you'll notice ruins for what used to be a barn and milk house as well as a side trail that leads to the foundation of an old farmhouse. Through the first half of the 20th century, the recreation center was a working, privately-owned farm.

From the group area, take the Spring Trail south. If standing at the group area's center and looking west, you'll notice one trail runs directly west; to its left, a trail heads southwest, then to its left going straight south is the Spring Trail. The Spring Trail is largely a grassy, mowed area.

In about 0.2 miles, go on the trail heading directly west. You'll enter the recreation center's forested area. Bring along a tree guide and see if you identify the many northern hardwoods along the trail. Among them are ash, basswood, maple, oak, white birch, and yellow birch.

At the next junction, in about 0.07 miles, go right/north. Watch for the lean-tos built on the trail's right side. Every year, hundreds of elementary and middle school students visit the site to learn about nature, a tradition since the early 1970s when the school district purchased the forest from Ed Bjornson of the Spring Valley Lumber Company. Keep an eye out for lost mittens.

The trail loops back west. At the next junction, in about 0.25 miles, go right/north. You'll cross two bridges, the first of which goes over a stream feeding Hay Creek and the second of which is Hay Creek. Several strong springs in the surrounding hillsides feed the waterway.

In about 0.07 miles, you'll reach the next junction, a logging road. Go right/east. Profits from timber sales at the school forest pay for the facility and environmental education in the district. Students also plant trees here and collect acorns for state tree nurseries.

The logging road runs past towering red pines and alongside the ever gurgling Hay Creek, then after about a third of a mile reaches the main group area. From there, follow the entrance road back to your vehicle.

Chippewa River State Trail

The spirits of children, a dead high school prom queen, and hellhounds await night hikers on a segment of the Chippewa River State Trail south of Menomonie.

Tucked in the southwest corner of Dunn County may be one of the Midwest's most haunted regions. A 5-mile round trip hike through the Chippewa River swamps offers just a small sample of those specters.

To reach the trail, from Wis. Hwy. 85 between Eau Claire and Durand, turn north onto County Road O. Upon entering the crossroads town of Meridean, continue past 160th Avenue onto the dirt Ferry Road. Park at its terminus, the site of the former Meridean boat landing.

Mary Dean

The spirit of a young girl named Mary Dean, who the village is named after, allegedly haunts the landing. She died on a ship traversing the river and was buried nearby. These days, the girl's ghost allegedly tries to encourage passersby to save her. Like the Greek Sirens of old, though, her goal is to lead you to a watery grave.

Walk Ferry Road back to the Chippewa River State Trail, turning left/northeast into farmland. Should the local farmer have planted corn, listen closely for the sound of laughing children. Several stories have been told of ghosts of children playing in corn fields across the area.

And when entering wooded areas, keep a watch for hellhounds – ethereal, black dogs with glowing red dogs – whose snarls and howls allegedly have been heard here.

At the 1.7-mile mark, the trail veers east, paralleling a back channel of the river. Keep a lookout for headlights gazing up at you from the water. An intoxicated high school prom queen allegedly drowned in the river after driving her car into it.

Ghosts of running children

Atop the hill across the river is Sand Hill Cemetery. About 20 graves there is the last resting place of people who died on nearby Meridean Island. Ghosts of running children have been seen in the fields around the cemetery. Others have reported balls of light hovering over the cemetery or hearing their names called from it. And those hellhounds are there, too.

Among the other supernatural legends in the area are a schoolhouse haunted by a boy who allegedly froze to death there and of a haunted church in nearby Caryville where a priest hung himself. Both of those stories appear to be apocryphal, however.

At the 2.5 mile mark, the trail comes to shoreline of back-channel for the Chippewa River. This marks a good spot to turn around.

Be careful when driving back to civilization, though. Remember that drowned prom queen? Sometimes she plays chicken with drivers, her phantom headlights heading right for you then disappearing just before smashing into your vehicle.

• Also see entries for this trail in the Eau Claire and Pepin counties sections.

Lower Chippewa River State Natural Area footpath

Lower Chippewa River State Natural Area

Day hikers can explore a rare savanna and prairie at the Lower Chippewa River State Natural Area.

The state natural area actually consists of several disconnected sites along the Chippewa River, stretching across three counties. Many of those sites are inaccessible, but one interesting area than can be walked is northwest of Caryville and makes for an interesting 0.4-miles round trip hike.

To reach the trailhead, from Wis. Hwy. 85 in Caryville, take County Road H north. Turn left/west into the state natural area's parking lot; if you cross the Chippewa River bridge, you've driven too far.

While there's no designated trail, an out-and-back footpath through the sand prairie and oak openings runs straight from the parking lot's southwest corner to a small, sparse grove of trees; simply follow the line of the tallest trees in the grass to the grove about 0.2 miles from the lot.

When Europeans first arrived in Wisconsin, the state has more than 7.7 million acres of native prairie; most of it was plowed under for fields or built on for homes. Today, a mere 8000 acres remain.

The Lower Chippewa River State Natural Areas aim to preserve Wisconsin's few remaining prairies and savannas along the Lower Chippewa River. They contain a full 25 percent of Wisconsin's existing prairies and savannas.

Such state natural areas protect a wide range of disappearing animals. In fact, six state-threatened species – the Acadian flycatcher, cerulean, hooded and Kentucky warblers, red-shouldered hawk, and yellow-crowned night heron – all can be found in the Lower Chippewa River State Natural Area. It is one of three places remaining in the world where the endangered Pecatonica River mayfly still exists. Meanwhile, the rare blue suckers, crystal darters, goldeyes, and the paddlefish prefer sections of the Chippewa and Red Cedar rivers next to prairies and savannas.

Upon reaching the grove, turn back for the parking lot.

A segment of the Chippewa River State Trail also runs along the southern edge of the same state natural area.

Other Dunn County Trails

• **Big Beaver Meadow State Natural Area trails** – A 0.6-

mile round trip jeep trail runs through an intriguing area of wet prairie and sedge meadow in which plants common to northern and to southern Wisconsin mix. The trailhead is located on 280th Street about a half-mile south of 1210th Avenue.

• **Bolen Creek State Hunting Grounds trails** – If you don't mind bushwhacking a little, you can amble through a typical Wisconsin woodlands here. Park on the side of 1270th Street at the northwest corner of the public lands for a walk to Bolen Creek, a Class II trout stream.

• **Caddie Woodlawn Historical Park walking paths** – The pioneer homestead home of the girl who inspired the 1935 Newbery Medal for children's literature is preserved off of Wis. Hwy. 25 about nine miles south of Menomonie. No formal paths exist, but there's plenty of space to walk about between a log cabin to a more modern farmhouse.

• **Dunnville Wildlife Area Trail** – A number of trails cut across the expansive Dunnville Wildlife Area between the Red Cedar and Chippewa rivers in southern Dunn County; a scenic one to take starts at the end of 580th Street (east of County Road Y); from the parking lot, head south on the jeep trail briefly through a woods then an open grassy area for a 0.95-mile round trip.

• **Eau Galle River Wildlife Area Loop** – A jeep trail loops 0.5 miles through a grassy area of the wildlife area to the shallow Eau Galle River which flows into the Chippewa River. Park at the trailhead on the east side of County Road C where it curves northeast of the junction with 150th Avenue. The property was formerly known as the Eau Galle River State Public Hunting Grounds.

• **Galloway Creek Trail** – Not an official trail, the 1-mile round trip hike at Menomonie Senior High School runs beneath the telephone poles off of Fifth Street West just south of Galloway Creek, hooks south to run along the Red Cedar

River, and ends on the west side of the school's practice fields. Streetside parking is available at the trailhead.

• **Hay Creek State Wildlife Area trails** – Park in the lot north of the Hwy. 64 and 810th Street junction; a trail heads through woodland to a wetlands as closing on Hay Creek. The waterflow flows west to east through the public land.

• **Junction Trail** – The former rail line turned hiking trail runs between the city library and Oak Avenue on the north side of Menomonie. Park along Oak Avenue east of North Broadway.

• **Menomonie Dog Park trails** – Dog owners can take Rex and Queenie on a variety of walking trails at the 11-acre park off of Brickyard Road north of Wis. Hwy. 29. Dogs must have license and a dog park tag (the latter is available at a park kiosk near the entrance).

• **Otter Creek Oak Barrens State Natural Area trails** – Bring a topo map for a little bushwhacking through an oak barrens that will impress. The large black oaks are at least 140 years old and may date to the 1810s while the smaller oaks are 70-110 years old. Access it from 1150th Avenue, where it curves north (east of County Road S); take jeep trail that zags about 0.6 miles to the public land's northern edge.

• **Stokke Trail** – The mile-long trail in Menomonie heads alongside a cascades-filled section of the Red Cedar River between Riverside Park off of Wis. Hwy. 29 (where there's parking) and Second Street NW near the dam that holds back the river to form Lake Menomin.

Eastern Pepin County

The Chippewa River splits the northern section of Pepin County in half then forms its eastern border and drains into the Mississippi River. A small county, the majority of its day hiking trails are located along or near the Chippewa. Most notably is the southern/western term-inus of the Chippewa River State Trail is in Durand. Trails in this section are listed from north to south.

Chippewa River State Trail segment
City of Durand

An old railroad bed now provides an excellent opportunity for day hiking in Pepin County.

The Chippewa River State Trail runs 30 miles from Durand to Eau Claire. It connects to the Red Cedar State Trail, which heads to Menomonie, and plans are underway to link it to the Old Abe State Trail in Chippewa Falls, creating the Chippewa Valley Trail System.

In Pepin County, 6.75 miles of the trail heads from downtown Durand across the county line to the Red Cedar State Trail junction. For day hikers, that's a long walk, but it can be split into shorter and more manageable segments.

Begin by parking at Durand's Tarrant Park, which is off of Wis. Hwy. 85 north of 14th Avenue East. The trail is directly north of the parking lot.

Starting there makes for easy parking and cuts 0.75 miles off the hike by eliminating the trail section that runs to downtown.

In the park, take the trail northeast. Though trees line the walkway, you'll still catch a number of good views of fields and dairy farms.

In 0.9 miles, you'll reach Bear Creek, a tributary to the

Chippewa River. The trail there becomes increasingly wooded as heading toward the Chippewa.

As a former Milwaukee Road railroad line, the grade generally is flat and even, originally built to ensure trains were as fuel efficient as possible.

About 0.6 miles from the creek, the trail crosses the Bear Lake Bridge over a wetlands that sits at the tip of a branch of the Chippewa River. During spring, the water typically is higher and bluer than in late summer.

The trail remains fairly wooded for the next 1.7 miles until reaching Hurlburt Lane. This marks a good spot to turn around for a 6.4-mile round trip (3.2-miles one-way) hike.

Red Cedar State Trail Junction to
Hubbard's Landing segment

Another way to hike the trail in Pepin County is to start across the county line at the nearest parking lot north of Durand.

That segment begins near the trail's junction with the Red Cedar State Trail in Dunn County. Park in a turnaround lot off of 50th Avenue west of Weber Road/630th Street. Cross the road, heading northwest to the Chippewa River State Trail.

The Red Cedar trail junction actually is northeast of the lot, and if you've got some extra energy, the short walk (0.8-miles round trip) to that junction and the Red Cedar trail's bridge over the Chippewa River is worth the effort.

Otherwise, go left/southwest onto the Chippewa River State Trail for a walk through the woods. Maples, oaks and other Northern hardwoods dominate the forest.

In 0.8 miles, the trail reaches Prissel Lane. After that, the terrain turns to fertile farmland.

County Road M marks the county line. Upon reaching where the road swerves east, about 0.7 miles from Prissel Lane, you've entered Pepin County.

After another 0.6 miles, the trail actually crosses County Road M. Rather than continue south, head west down the shoulder of the county road for 0.3 miles to Hubbard's Landing on the Chippewa River's shores. There you'll spot sandbars where the river turns.

Head back the way you came to the parking lot for a 4.8-mile round trip (5.6 miles if adding the Red Cedar State Trail bridge).

• Also see entries for this trail in the Eau Claire and Dunn counties sections.

Silver Birch Park Trail
Silver Birch Park

Day hikers can enjoy a walk alongside a lake and through the woods on the Silver Birch Park Trail southwest of Durand.

The 0.6-mile round trip trail runs through Silver Birch Park to Holden Park Campground.

To reach the trail, from Durand, head west on Wis. Hwy. 25. Upon crossing the Chippewa River, turn left/south onto County Road P. Go left/south onto Silver Birch Road. At County Road NN/Round Hill Road, turn right/west. The next left/south is the park entry road. Use the parking spaces near the boat ramp.

Before hitting the trail, take a walk across the picnic area to Silver Birch Lake. As if it were a mirror, the lake impressively reflects the blue sky and clouds on days when the wind is low. The reflection seems to stretch forever – not surprisingly as the lake's surface area covers 145 acres and contains two small islands. The lake is popular with fishermen as it offers catfish, largemouth bass, northern pike, walleye and a variety of panfish.

For the walking path, head to the picnic area's north side and follow the paved road east. Where the road forks, go right/southwest.

You'll soon come to a walking path that cuts right/west between two fences. Take that path. After a bit, a tree canopy covers the route, which makes for a nice autumn walk when leaves change color.

Upon reaching the next asphalt road, you've arrived at Holden Park Campground. This marks a good spot to turn back.

The area surrounding and including Silver Birch Park is remarkably flat. That's because it is an outwash plain formed some 8000-12,000 years ago at the end of the last ice age. As glaciers melted, the water flowed southward in broad sheets centered on the nearby Chippewa River. It dropped sand and other sediment across the ground as leveling out the terrain.

Tiffany Bottoms State Wildlife Area trails
Tiffany Bottoms State Wildlife Area

The broad floodplains along the Chippewa River as it flows into the Mississippi River means it's easier to traverse by boat than foot. Still, three primitive trails in the Tiffany Bottoms State Wildlife Area give some access to this unique and interesting wilderness.

The 13,000-acre wildlife area stretches alongside both sides of the Chippewa River just south of Durand to the Mississippi. It is one of Wisconsin's largest continuous bottom-land hardwood forests.

Because of the protected space's vastness, a variety of wildlife are able to call the bottomlands home. Among them are beaver, otter, muskrat, raccoon, ruffed grouse, wood ducks, and whitetail deer. It's also a great area to spot several endangered and threatened species, including bald eagles, great egrets, red-shouldered hawks, Blanding's turtle, and the massasauga rattlesnake.

In Pepin County, on the Chippewa River's west side, two

trails run through the wildlife area.

The **Swede Ramble Trail** runs about 4-miles one-way through a meadow and the bottomland hardwood forest. Start at the parking lot off of Swede Rambler Lane southeast of Little Plum Creek and end at another lot off of Tulip Lane east of Big Hill Road. A couple of spur trails run west off of the main trail.

South of that area is the **Five-Mile Bluff Prairie Trail**, which runs about 3-miles total. From a parking lot at the end of 16th Creek Road, the trail heads north at the base of Five Mile Bluff then loops to and over its top, which is more than 300 feet above the river.

On the Buffalo County side of the Chippewa River, the **Thibodeau to Trevino Trail** rambles about 15 miles, often alongside various backwaters including a crossing of Buffalo Slough. For day hiking, a 10-mile round trip hike from the parking lot, off of Wis. Hwy. 25 just north of Thibodeau Road, to Buffalo Slough is a long enough route. If making it a point-to-point trail, the full trail ends at a boat ramp off of Wis. Hwy. 35 on the Chippewa's eastern shoreline.

Be forewarned that the trails are not marked, and especially during spring are prone to flooding. Always carry insect repellent with you and stay on the footpath.

Other Eastern Pepin County Trails

• **Laura Ingalls Wilder Wayside & Cabin walking paths** – About 0.1 miles of informal walking paths sit on a plot of land where famed writer Laura Ingalls Wilder spent the earliest years of her life, the Little Cabin in the Big Woods. The wayside, featuring a reconstructed log cabin, is on County Road CC, seven miles north of Wis. Hwy. 35 in rural Pepin.

• **Nine Mile Island State Natural Area Connector Trail** – A very primitive 0.6-mile round trip trail connects the natural area to the Chippewa River State Trail. Park in the state natural area's northern lot off of County Road M south of W. County Line Road. Oak barrens and floodplain forest dominate the state natural area.

Best Trails Lists

Which trails are the best for watching birds? To enjoy fall colors? Walking the family dog? Here are some lists of the best Chippewa Valley trails for those and many other specific interests.

Autumn leaves
- Eau Claire River Route
- River Road Ski Trail
- Tower Nature Trail

Birdwatching
- Circle Trail
- Putnam Trail State Natural Area
- Red Cedar State Trail

Campgrounds
- Beaver Meadow Nature Trail
- Coon Fork Lake Trail
- Silver Birch Park Trail

Dog-friendly
- Circle Trail
- Menomin Park Loop
- Menomonie Dog Park trails

Geology
- Big Falls Trail (Big Falls County Park)
- Circle Trail
- Devil's Punchbowl Trail
- Irvine Park Loop

Haunted
• Chippewa River State Trail, Meridean boat landing segment
• Devil's Punchbowl Trail

History/Archeology
• Caddie Woodlawn Historical Park walking paths
• Lake Trail (effigy mounds)
• Laura Ingalls Wilder Wayside & Cabin walking paths
• Paul Bunyan Logging Camp Museum walking path

Must-do's
• Chippewa River State Trail, Water Street to Phoenix Park
• Jean Brunet Nature Trail
• Lake Trail
• Old Abe State Trail, Jim Falls to south of Cobban segment
• Red Cedar State Trail, Riverside Park to Devil's Punchbowl

Observation towers
• Mound Park Castle Trail
• Tower Nature Trail

Picnicking
• Big Falls Trail (Big Falls County Park)
• Bjornson Education-Recreation Center Loop
• Circle Trail

Plant communities
• Eau Claire River Route
• Jean Brunet Nature Trail
• Timber Trail
• Tower Nature Trail

Primitive trails
• Ice Age National Scenic Trail, Deer Fly Trail Area

- Elk Mound Swamp trails
- Thibodeau to Trevino Trail

Rivers
- Chippewa River State Trail
- Old Abe State Trail
- Red Cedar State Trail

Vistas
- Five-Mile Bluff Prairie Trail
- River Road Ski Trail
- Tower Nature Trail

Waterfalls
- Big Falls Trail (Big Falls County Park)
- Devil's Punchbowl Trail

Wildflowers
- Prairie Wildflower Nature Trail
- Wildflower Trail

Wildlife
- Augusta Wildlife Area Trail
- Catherine Hoffman Hartl Memorial Wetland Trail
- Jean Brunet Nature Trail
- Putnam State Natural Area trails
- River Road Ski Trail

Bonus Section: Day Hiking Primer

You'll get more out of a day hike if you research it and plan ahead. It's not enough to just pull over to the side of the road and hit a trail that you've never been on and have no idea where it goes. In fact, doing so invites disaster.

Instead, you should preselect a trail (This book's trail descriptions can help you do that). You'll also want to ensure that you have the proper clothing, equipment, navigational tools, first-aid kit, food and water. Knowing the rules of the trail and potential dangers along the way also are helpful. In this special section, we'll look at each of these topics to ensure you're fully prepared.

Selecting a Trail

For your first few hikes, stick to short, well-known trails where you're likely to encounter others. Once you get a feel for hiking, your abilities, and your interests, expand to longer and more remote trails.

Always check to see what the weather will be like on the trail you plan to hike. While an adult might be able to withstand wind and a sprinkle here or there, for kids it can be pure misery. Dry, pleasantly warm days with limited wind always are best when hiking with children.

Don't choose a trail that is any longer than the least fit person in your group can hike. Adults in good shape can go 8-12 miles a day; for kids, it's much less. There's no magical number.

When planning the hike, try to find a trail with a mid-point payoff – that is something you and definitely any children will find exciting about half-way through the hike. This will help keep up everyone's energy and enthusiasm during the journey.

If you have children in your hiking party, consider a couple of additional points when selecting a trail.

Until children enter their late teens, they need to stick to trails rather than going off-trail hiking, which is known as bushwhacking. Children too easily can get lost when off trail. They also can easily get scratched and cut up or stumble across poisonous plants and dangerous animals.

Generally, kids will prefer a circular route to one that requires hiking back the way you came. The return trip often feels anti-climatic, but you can overcome that by mentioning features that all of you might want to take a closer look at.

Once you select a trail, it's time to plan for your day hike. Doing so will save you a lot of grief – and potentially prevent an emergency – later on. You are, after all, entering the wilds, a place where help may not be readily available.

When planning your hike, follow these steps:

• Print a road map showing how to reach the parking lot near the trailhead. Outline the route with a transparent yellow highlighter and write out the directions.

• Print a satellite photo of the parking area and the trailhead. Mark the trailhead on the photo.

• Print a topo map of the trail. Outline the trail with the yellow highlighter. Note interesting features you want to see along the trail and the destination.

• If carrying GPS, program this information into your device.

• Make a timeline for your trip, listing: when you will leave home; when you will arrive at the trailhead; your turn back time; when you will return for home in your vehicle; and when you will arrive at your home.

• Estimate how much water and food you will need to bring based on the amount of time you plan to spend on the trail and in your vehicle. You'll need at least two pints of water per person for every hour on the trail.

• Fill out two copies of a hiker's safety form. Leave one in your vehicle.

• Share all of this information with a responsible person remaining in civilization, leaving a hiker's safety form with them. If they do not hear from you within an hour of when you plan to leave the trail in your vehicle, they should contact authorities to report you as possibly lost.

Clothing
Footwear

If your feet hurt, the hike is over, so getting the right footwear is worth the time. Making sure the footwear fits before hitting the trail also is worth it. With children, if you've gone a few weeks without hiking, that's plenty of time for feet to grow, and they may have just outgrown their hiking boots. Check out everyone's footwear a few days before heading out on the hike. If it doesn't fit, replace it.

For flat, smooth, dry trails, sneakers and cross-trainers are fine; but if you really want to head onto less traveled roads or tackle areas that aren't typically dry, you'll need hiking boots. Once you start doing any rocky or steep trails – and remember that a trail you consider moderately steep needs to be only half that angle for a child to consider it extremely steep – you'll want hiking boots, which offer rugged tread perfect for handling rough trails.

Socks

Socks serve two purposes: to wick sweat away from skin and to provide cushioning. Cotton socks aren't very good for hiking, except in extremely dry environments, because they retain moisture that can lead to blisters. Wool socks or liner socks work best. You'll want to look for three-season socks, also known as trekking socks. While a little thicker than summer socks, their extra cushioning generally prevents blisters.

Also, make sure kids don't put on holey socks; that's just inviting blisters.

Layering

On all but the hot, dry days, when hiking you should wear multiple layers of clothing that provide various levels of protection against sweat, heat loss, wind and potentially rain. Layering works because the type of clothing you select for each stratum serves a different function, such as wicking moisture or shielding against wind. In addition, trapped air between each layer of clothing is warmed by your body heat. Layers also can be added or taken off as needed.

Generally, you need three layers. Closest to your skin is the wicking layer, which pulls perspiration away from the body and into the next layer, where it evaporates. Exertion from walking means you will sweat and generate heat, even if the weather is cold. The second layer provides insulation, which helps keep you warm. The last layer is a water-resistant shell that protects you from rain, wind, snow and sleet.

As the seasons and weather change, so does the type of clothing you select for each layer. The first layer ought to be a loose-fitting T-shirt in summer, but in winter and on other cold days you might opt for a long-sleeved moisture-wicking synthetic material, like polypropylene. During winter, the next layer probably also should cover the neck, which often is exposed to the elements. A turtleneck works fine, but preferably not one made of cotton. The third layer in winter, depending on the temperature, could be a wool sweater, a half-zippered long sleeved fleece jacket, or a fleece vest.

You might even add a fourth layer of a hooded parka with pockets, made of material that can block wind and resist water. Gloves or mittens as well as a hat also are necessary on cold days.

Headgear

Half of all body heat is lost through the head, hence the hiker's adage, "If your hands are cold, wear a hat." In cool, wet weather, wearing a hat is at least good for avoiding hypothermia, a potentially deadly condition in which heat loss occurs faster than the body can generate it. Children are more susceptible to hypothermia than adults.

Especially during summer, a hat with a wide brim is useful in keeping the sun out of eyes. It's also nice should rain start falling.

For young children, get a hat with a chin strap. They like to play with their hats, which will fly off in a wind gust if not fastened some way to the child.

Sunglasses

Sunglasses are an absolute must if walking through open areas exposed to the sun and in winter when you can suffer from snow blindness. Look for 100% UV-protective shades, which provide the best screen.

Equipment

A couple of principles should guide your purchases. First, the longer and more complex the hike, the more equipment you'll need. Secondly, your general goal is to go light. Since you're on a day hike, the amount of gear you'll need is a fraction of what backpackers shown in magazines and catalogues usually carry. Still, the inclination of most day hikers is to not carry enough equipment. For the lightness issue, most gear today is made with titanium and siliconized nylon, ensuring it is sturdy yet fairly light. While the following list of what you need may look long, it won't weigh much.

Backpacks

Sometimes called daypacks (for day hikes or for kids),

backpacks are essential to carry all of the essentials you need – snacks, first-aid kit, extra clothing.

For day hiking, you'll want to get yourself an internal frame, in which the frame giving the backpack its shape is inside the pack's fabric so it's not exposed to nature. Such frames usually are lightweight and comfortable. External frames have the frame outside the pack, so they are exposed to the elements. They are excellent for long hikes into the backcountry when you must carry heavy loads.

As kids get older, and especially after they've been hiking for a couple of years, they'll want a "real" backpack. Unfortunately, most backpacks for kids are overbuilt and too heavy. Even light ones that safely can hold up to 50 pounds are inane for most children.

When buying a daypack for your child, look for sternum straps, which help keep the strap on the shoulders. This is vital for prepubescent children, as they do not have the broad shoulders that come with adolescence, meaning packs likely will slip off and onto their arms, making them uncomfortable and difficult to carry. Don't buy a backpack that a child will "grow into." Backpacks that don't fit well simply will lead to sore shoulder and back muscles and could result in poor posture.

Also, consider purchasing a daypack with a hydration system for kids. This will help ensure they drink a lot of water. More on this later when we get to canteens.

Before hitting the trail, always check your children's backpacks to make sure that they have not overloaded them. Kids think they need more than they really do. They also tend to overestimate their own ability to carry stuff. Sibling rivalries often lead to children packing more than they should in their rucksacks, too. Don't let them overpack "to teach them a lesson," though, as it can damage bones and turn the hike into a bad experience.

A good rule of thumb is no more than 25 percent capacity. Most upper elementary school kids can carry only about 10 pounds for any short distance. Subtract the weight of the backpack, and that means only 4-5 pounds in the backpack. Overweight children will need to carry a little less than this or they'll quickly be out of breath.

Child carriers

If your child is an infant or toddler, you'll have to carry him. Until infants can hold their heads up, which usually doesn't happen until about four to six months of age, a front pack (like a Snugli or Baby Bjorn) is best. It keeps the infant close for warmth and balances out your backpack. At the same time, though, you must watch for baby overheating in a front pack, so you'll need to remove the infant from your body at rest stops.

Once children reach about 20 pounds, they typically can hold their heads up and sit on their own. At that point, you'll want a baby carrier (sometimes called a child carrier or baby backpack), which can transfer the infant's weight to your hips when you walk. You'll not only be comfortable, but your child will love it, too.

Look for a baby carrier that is sturdy yet lightweight. Your child is going to get heavier as time passes, so about the only way you can counteract this is to reduce the weight of the items you use to carry things. The carrier also should have adjustment points, as you don't want your child to outgrow the carrier too soon. A padded waist belt and padded should-er straps are necessary for your comfort. The carrier should provide some kind of head and neck support if you're hauling an infant. It also should offer back support for children of all ages, and leg holes should be wide enough so there's no chafing. You want to be able to load your infant without help, so it should be stable enough to stand that way when you take it off the child can sit in it for a moment while you get turned around. Stay away from baby carriers with only shoulder straps as you need the waist belt to help shift the child's weight to your hips for more comfortable walking.

Fanny packs

Also known as a belt bag, a fanny pack is virtually a must for anyone with a baby carrier as you can't otherwise lug a backpack. If your significant other is with you, he or she can carry the backpack, of course. Still, the fanny pack also is a good alternative to a backpack in hot weather, as it will reduce back sweat.

If you have only one or two kids on a hike, or if they also are old enough to carry daypacks, your fanny pack need not be large. A mid-size pouch can carry at least 200 cubic inches of supplies, which is more than enough to accommodate all the materials you need. A good fanny pack also has a spot for hooking canteens to.

Canteens

Canteens or plastic bottles filled with water are vital for any hike, no matter how short the trail. You'll need to have enough of them to carry about two pints of water per person for every hour of hiking.

Trekking poles

Also known as walking poles or walking sticks, trekking poles are necessary for maintaining stability on uneven or wet surfaces and to help reduce fatigue. The latter makes them useful on even surfaces. By transferring weight to the arms, a trekking pole can reduce stress on knees and lower back, allowing you to maintain a better posture and to go farther.

If an adult with a baby or toddler on your back, you'll primarily want a trekking pole to help you maintain your balance, even if on a flat surface, and to help absorb some of the impact of your step.

Graphite tips provide the best traction. A basket just above the tip is a good idea so the stick doesn't sink into mud or sand. Angled cork handles are ergonomic and help absorb sweat from your hands so they don't blister. A strap on the handle to wrap around your hand is useful so the stick doesn't slip out. Telescopic poles are a good idea as you can adjust them as needed based on the terrain you're hiking and as kids grow to accommodate their height.

The pole also needs to be sturdy enough to handle rugged terrain, as you don't want a pole that bends when you press it to the ground. Spring-loaded shock absorbers help when heading down a steep incline but aren't necessary. Indeed, for a short walk across flat terrain, the right length stick is about all you need.

Carabiners

Carabiners are metal loops, vaguely shaped like a D, with a sprung or screwed gate. You'll find that hooking a couple of them to your backpack or fanny pack useful in many ways. For example, if you need to dig through a fanny pack, you can hook the strap of your trekking pole to it. Your hat, camera straps, first-aid kit, and a number of other objects also can connect to them. Hook carabiners to your fanny pack or backpack upon purchasing them so you don't forget them when packing. Small carabiners with sprung gates are inexpensive, but they do have a limited life span of a couple of dozen hikes.

Navigational Tools
Paper maps

Paper maps may sound passé in this age of GPS, but you'll

find the variety and breadth of view they offer to be useful. During the planning process, a paper map (even if viewing it online), will be far superior to a GPS device. On the hike, you'll also want a backup to GPS. Or like many casual hikers, you may not own GPS at all, which makes paper maps indispensable.

Standard road maps (which includes printed guides and handmade trail maps) show highways and locations of cities and parks. Maps included in guidebooks, printed guides handed out at parks, and those that are hand-drawn tend to be designed like road maps, and often carry the same positives and negatives.

Topographical maps give contour lines and other important details for crossing a landscape. You'll find them invaluable on a hike into the wilds. The contour lines' shape and their spacing on a topo map show the form and steepness of a hill or bluff, unlike the standard road map and most brochures and hand-drawn trail maps. You'll also know if you're in a woods, which is marked in green, or in a clearing, which is marked in white. If you get lost, figuring out where you are and how to get to where you need to be will be much easier with such information.

Satellite photos offer a view from above that is rendered exactly as it would look from an airplane. Thanks to Google and other online services, you can get fairly detailed pictures of the landscape. Such pictures are an excellent resource when researching a hiking trail. Unfortunately, those pictures don't label what a feature is or what it's called, as would a topo map. Unless there's a stream, determining if a feature is a valley bottom or a ridgeline also can be difficult. Like topo maps, satellite photos can be out of date a few years.

GPS

By using satellites, the global positioning system can find

your spot on the Earth to within 10 feet. With a GPS device, you can preprogram the trailhead location and mark key turns and landmarks as well as the hike's end point. This mobile map is a powerful technological tool that almost certainly ensures you won't get lost – so long as you've correctly programmed the information. GPS also can calculate travel time and act as a compass, a barometer and altimeter, making such devices virtually obsolete on a hike.

In remote areas, however, reception is spotty at best for GPS, rendering your mobile map worthless. A GPS device also runs on batteries, and there's always a chance they will go dead. Or you may drop your device, breaking it in the process. Their screens are small, and sometimes you need a large paper map to get a good sense of the natural landmarks around you.

Compass

Like a paper map, a compass is indispensable even if you use GPS. Should your GPS no longer function, the compass then can be used to tell you which direction you're heading. A protractor compass is best for hiking. Beneath the compass needle is a transparent base with lines to help your orient yourself. The compass often serves as a magnifying glass to help you make out map details. Most protractor compasses also come with a lanyard for easy carrying.

Food and Water
Water

As water is the heaviest item you'll probably carry, there is a temptation to not take as much as one should. Don't skimp on the amount of water you bring, though; after all, it's the one supply your body most needs. It's always better to end up having more water than you needed than returning to your vehicle dehydrated.

How much water should you take? Adults need at least a quart for every two hours hiking. Children need to drink about a quart every two hours of walking and more if the weather is hot or dry. To keep kids hydrated, have them drink at every rest stop.

Don't presume there will be water on the hiking trail. Most trails outside of urban areas lack such amenities. In addition, don't drink water from local streams, lakes, rivers or ponds. There's no way to tell if local water is safe or not. As soon as you have consumed half of your water supply, you should turn around for the vehicle.

Food

Among the many wonderful things about hiking is that snacking between meals isn't frowned upon. Unless going on an all-day hike in which you'll picnic along the way, you want to keep everyone in your hiking party fed, especially as hunger can lead to lethargic and discontented children. It'll also keep young kids from snacking on the local flora or dirt. Before hitting the trail, you'll want to repackage as much of the food as possible as products sold at grocery stores tend to come in bulky packages that take up space and add a little weight to your backpack. Place the food in re-sealable plastic bags.

Bring a variety of small snacks for rest stops. You don't want kids filling up on snacks, but you do need them to maintain their energy levels if they're walking or to ensure they don't turn fussy if riding in a child carrier. Go for complex carbohydrates and proteins for maintaining energy. Good options include dried fruits, jerky, nuts, peanut butter, prepared energy bars, candy bars with a high protein content (nuts, peanut butter), crackers, raisins and trail mix (called "gorp"). A number of trail mix recipes are available online (*hikeswithtykes.blogspot.com/search?q=trail+mix+recipe*);

you and your children may want to try them out at home to see which ones you collectively like most.

Salty treats rehydrate better than sweet treats do. Chocolate and other sweets are fine if they're not all that's exclusively served, but remember they also tend to lead to thirst and to make sticky messes. Whichever snacks you choose, don't experiment with food on the trail. Bring what you know kids will like.

Give the first snack within a half-hour of leaving the trailhead or you risk children becoming tired and whiny from low energy levels. If kids start asking for them every few steps even after having something to eat at the last rest stop, consider timing snacks to reaching a seeable landmark, such as, "We'll get out the trail mix when we reach that bend up ahead."

Milk for infants

If you have an infant or unweaned toddler with you, milk is as necessary as water. Children who only drink breastfed milk but don't have their mother on the hike require that you have breast-pumped milk in an insulated beverage container (such as a Thermos) that can keep it cool to avoid spoiling. Know how much the child drinks and at what frequency so you can bring enough. You'll also need to carry the child's bottle and feeding nipples. Bring enough extra water in your canteen so you can wash out the bottle after each feeding. A handkerchief can be used to dry bottles between feedings.

Don't forget a pacifier. Make sure it has a string and hook attached so it connects to the baby's outfit and isn't lost.

What not to bring

Avoid soda and other caffeinated beverages, alcohol, and energy pills. The caffeine will dehydrate children as well as you. Alcohol has no place on the trail; you need your full faculties when making decisions and driving home. Energy pills essentially are a stimulant and like alcohol can lead to bad calls. If you're tired, get some sleep and hit the trail another day.

First-aid Kit
>After water, this is the most essential item you can carry. A first-aid kit should include:
>- Adhesive bandages of various types and sizes, especially butterfly bandages (for younger kids, make sure they're colorful kid bandages)
>- Aloe vera
>- Anesthetic (such as Benzocaine)
>- Antacid (tablets)
>- Antibacterial (aka antibiotic) ointment (such as Neosporin or Bacitracin)
>- Anti-diarrheal tablets (for adults only, as giving this to a child is controversial)
>- Anti-itch cream or calamine lotion
>- Antiseptics (such as hydrogen peroxide, iodine or Betadine, Mercuroclear, rubbing alcohol)
>- Baking soda
>- Breakable (or instant) ice packs
>- Cotton swabs
>- Disposable syringe (w/o needle)
>- Epipen (if children or adults have allergies)
>- Fingernail clippers (your multi-purpose tool might have this, and if so you can dispense with it)
>- Gauze bandage
>- Gauze compress pads (2x2 individually wrapped pad)
>- Hand sanitizer (use this in place of soap)
>- Liquid antihistamine (not Benadryl tablets, however, as children should take liquid not pills; be aware that liquid antihistamines may cause drowsiness)

- Medical tape
- Moisturizer containing an anti-inflammatory
- Mole skin
- Pain reliever (aka aspirin; for children's pain relief, use liquid acetaminophen such Tylenol or liquid ibuprofen; never give aspirin to a child under 12)
- Poison ivy cream (for treatment)
- Poison ivy soap
- Powdered sports drinks mix or electrolyte additives
- Sling
- Snakebite kit
- Thermometer
- Tweezers (your multi-purpose tool may have this allowing you to dispense with it)
- Water purification tablets

If infants are with you, be sure to also carry teething ointment (such as Orajel) and diaper rash treatment.

Many of the items should be taken out of their store packaging to make placement in your fanny pack or backpack easier. In addition, small amounts of some items – such as baking soda and cotton swabs – can be placed inside re-sealable plastic bags, since you won't need the whole amount purchased.

Make sure the first-aid items are in a waterproof container. A re-sealable plastic zipper bag is perfectly fine. As the Chippewa Valley sports a humid climate, be sure to replace the adhesive bandages every couple of months, as they can deteriorate in the moistness. Also, check your first-aid kit every few trips and after any hike in which you've just used it, so that you can replace used components and to make sure medicines haven't expired.

If you have older elementary-age kids and teenagers who've been trained in first aid, giving them a kit to carry as well as yourself is a good idea. Should they find themselves lost or if you cannot get to them for a few moments, the kids might need to provide very basic first aid to one another.

Hiking with Children: Attitude Adjustment

To enjoy hiking with kids, you'll first have to adopt your child's perspective. Simply put, we must learn to hike on our kids' schedules – even though they may not know that's what we're doing.

Compared to adults, kids can't walk as far, they can't walk as fast, and they will grow bored more quickly. Every step we take requires three for them. In addition, early walkers, up to two years of age, prefer to wander than to "hike." Preschool kids will start to walk the trail, but at a rate of only about a mile per hour. With stops, that can turn a three-mile hike into a four-hour journey. Kids also won't be able to hike as steep of trails as you or handle as inclement of weather as you might.

This all may sound limiting, especially to long-time back-packers used to racking up miles or bagging peaks on their hikes, but it's really not. While you may have to put off some backcountry and mountain climbing trips for a while, it also opens up to you a number of great short trails and nature hikes with spectacular sights that you may have otherwise skipped because they weren't challenging enough.

So sure, you'll have to make some compromises, but the payout is high. You're not personally on the hike to get a workout but to spend quality time with your children.

Family Dog

Dogs are part of the family, and if you have children, they'll want to share the hiking experience with their pets. In turn, dogs will have a blast on the trail, some larger dogs can be used as Sherpas, and others will defend against threatening animals.

But there is a downside to dogs. Many will chase animals and so run the risk of getting lost or injured. Also, a doggy bag will have to be carried for dog pooh – yeah, it's natural, but also inconsiderate to leave for other hikers to smell and for their kids to step in. In addition, most dogs almost always will lose a battle against a threatening animal, so there's a price to be paid for your safety.

Many places where you'll hike solve the dilemma for you as dogs aren't allowed on their trails. Dogs are verboten on some park trails but usually permitted on those in national forests. Always check with the park ranger before heading to the trail.

If you can bring a dog, make sure it is well behaved and friendly to others. You don't need your dog biting another hiker while unnecessarily defending its family.

Rules of the Trail

Ah, the woods or a wide open meadow, peaceful and quiet, not a single soul around for miles. Now you and your children can do whatever you want.

Not so fast.

Act like wild animals on a hike, and you'll destroy the very aspects of the wilds that make them so attractive. You're also likely to end up back in civilization, specifically an emergency room. And there are other people around. Just as you would wish them to treat you courte-ously, so you and your children should do the same for them.

Let's cover how to act civilized out in the wilds.

Minimize damage to your surroundings

When on the trail, follow the maxim of "Leave no trace." Obviously, you shouldn't toss litter on the ground, start rock-slides, or pollute water supplies. How much is damage and how much is good-natured exploring is a gray area, of course.

Most serious backpackers will say you should never pick up objects, break branches, throw rocks, pick flowers, and so on – the idea is not to disturb the environment at all.

Good luck getting a four-year-old to think like that. The good news is a four-year-old won't be able to throw around many rocks or break many branches.

Still, children from their first hike into the wilderness should be taught to respect nature and to not destroy their environment. While you might overlook a preschooler hurling rocks into a puddle, they can be taught to sniff rather than pick flowers. As they grow older, you can teach them the value of leaving the rock alone. Regardless of age, don't allow children to write on boulders or carve into trees.

Many hikers split over picking berries. To strictly abide by the "minimize damage" principle, you wouldn't pick any berries at all. Kids, however, are likely to find great pleasure in eating blackberries, currants and thimbleberries as ambling down the trail. Personally, I don't see any problem enjoying a few berries if the long-term payoff is a respect and love for nature. To minimize damage, teach them to only pick berries they can reach from the trail so they don't trample plants or deplete food supplies for animals. They also should only pick what they'll eat.

Collecting is another issue. In national and most state and county parks, taking rocks, flower blossoms and even pine cones is illegal. Picking flowers moves many species, especially if they are rare and native, one step closer to extinction. Archeological ruins are extremely fragile, and even touching them can damage a site.

But on many trails, especially gem trails, collecting is part of the adventure. Use common sense – if the point of the trail is to find materials to collect, such as a gem trail, take judiciously, meaning don't overcollect. Otherwise, leave it there.

Sometimes the trail crosses private land. If so, walking

around fields, not through them, always is best or you could damage a farmer's crops.

Pack out what you pack in

Set the example as a parent: Don't litter yourself; whenever stopping, pick up whatever you've dropped; and always require kids to pick up after themselves when they litter. In the spirit of "Leave no trace," try to leave the trail cleaner than you found it, so if you come across litter that's safe to pick up, do so and bring it back to a trash bin in civilization. Given this, you may want to bring a plastic bag to carry out garbage.

Picking up litter doesn't just mean gum and candy wrappers but also some organic materials that take a long time to decompose and aren't likely to be part of the natural environment you're hiking. In particular, these include peanut shells, orange peelings, and eggshells.

Burying litter, by the way, isn't viable. Either animals or erosion soon will dig it up, leaving it scattered around the trail and woods.

Stay on the trail

Hiking off trail means potentially damaging fragile growth. Following this rule not only ensures you minimize damage but is also a matter of safety. Off trail is where kids most likely will encounter dangerous animals and poisonous plants. Not being able to see where they're stepping also increases the likelihood of falling and injuring themselves. Leaving the trail raises the chances of getting lost. Staying on the trail also means staying out of caves, mines or abandoned structures you may encounter. They are usually dangerous places.

Finally, never let children take a shortcut on a switchback. Besides putting them on steep ground upon which they could slip, their impatient act will cause the switchback to erode.

Trail Dangers

On Chippewa Valley trails, two common dangers face hikers: ticks and poison ivy/sumac. Both can make miserable your time on the trail or once back home. Fortunately, both threats are easily avoidable and treatable.

Ticks

One of the greatest dangers comes from the smallest of creatures: ticks. Both the wood and the deer tick are common in the Chippewa Valley and can infect people with Lyme disease.

Ticks usually leap onto people from the top of a grass blade as you brush against it, so walking in the middle of the trail away from high plants is a good idea. Wearing a hat, a long sleeve shirt tucked into pants, and pants tucked into shoes or socks, also will keep ticks off you, though this is not foolproof as they sometimes can hook onto clothing. A tightly woven cloth provides the best protection, however. Children can pick up a tick that has hitchhiked onto the family dog, so outfit Rover and Queenie with a tick-repelling collar.

After hiking into an area where ticks live, you'll want to examine your children's bodies (as well as your own) for them. Check warm, moist areas of the skin, such as under the arms, the groin and head hair. Wearing light-colored clothing helps make the tiny tick easier to spot.

To get rid of a tick that has bitten your child, drip either disinfectant or rubbing alcohol on the bug, so it will loosen its grip. Grip the tick close to its head, slowly pulling it away from the skin. This hopefully will prevent it from releasing saliva that spreads disease. Rather than kill the tick, keep it in a plastic bag so that medical professionals can analyze it should disease symptoms appear. Next, wash the bite area with soap and water then apply antiseptic.

In the days after leaving the woods, also check for signs of disease from ticks. Look for bulls-eye rings, a sign of a Lyme disease. Other symptoms include a large red rash, joint pain, and flu-like symptoms. Indications of Rocky Mountain spotted fever include headache, fever, severe muscle aches, and a spotty rash first on palms and feet soles that spread, all beginning about two days after the bite.

If any of these symptoms appear, seek medical attention immediately. Fortunately, antibiotics exist to cure most tick-related diseases.

Poison ivy/sumac

Often the greatest danger in the wilds isn't our own clumsiness or foolhardiness but various plants we encounter. The good news is that we mostly have to force the encounter with flora. Touching the leaves of either poison ivy or poison sumac in particular results in an itchy, painful rash. Each plant's sticky resin, which causes the reaction, clings to clothing and hair, so you may not have "touched" a leaf, but once your hand runs against the resin on shirt or jeans, you'll probably get the rash.

To avoid touching these plants, you'll need to be able to identify each one. Remember the "Leaves of three, let it be" rule for poison ivy. Besides groups of three leaflets, poison ivy has shiny green leaves that are red in spring and fall. Poison sumac's leaves are not toothed as are non-poisonous sumac, and in autumn their leaves turn scarlet. Be forewarned that even after leaves fall off, poison oak's stems can carry some of the itchy resin.

By staying on the trail and walking down its middle rather than the edges, you are unlikely to come into contact with this pair of irritating plants. That probably is the best preventative. Poison ivy barrier creams also can be helpful, but they only temporarily block the resin. This lulls you into a false sense of safety, and so you may not bother to watch for poison ivy.

To treat poison ivy/sumac, wash the part of the body that has touched the plant with poison ivy soap and cold water. This will erode the oily resin, so it'll be easier to rinse off. If you don't have any of this special soap, plain soap sometimes will work if used within a half-hour of touching the plant. Apply a poison ivy cream and get medical attention immediately. Wearing gloves, remove any clothing (including shoes) that has touched the plants, washing them and the worn gloves right away.

For more about these topics and many others, pick up this author's **Hikes with Tykes: A Practical Guide to Day Hiking with Kids**. You also can find tips online at the author's **DayHikingTrails blog** (*hikeswithtykes.blogspot.com*). We'll see ya' on the trail!

Index

About the Author

Rob Bignell is a long-time hiker, journalist, and author of the popular "Hikes with Tykes," "Headin' to the Cabin," and "Hittin' the Trail" guidebooks and several other titles. He and his son Kieran have been hiking together for the past eight years. Before Kieran, Rob served as an infantryman in the Army National Guard and taught middle school students in New Mexico and Wisconsin. His newspaper work has won several national and state journalism awards, from editorial writing to sports reporting. In 2001, The Prescott Journal, which he served as managing editor of, was named Wisconsin's Weekly Newspaper of the Year. Rob and Kieran live in Wisconsin.

CHECK OUT THESE OTHER HIKING BOOKS BY ROB BIGNELL

"Best Sights to See" series:
◆America's National Parks
◆Great Smoky Mountains National Park

"Headin' to the Cabin" series:
◆Day Hiking Trails of Northeast Minnesota
◆Day Hiking Trails of Northwest Wisconsin

"Hikes with Tykes" series:
◆Hikes with Tykes: A Practical Guide to Day Hiking with
  Children
◆Hikes with Tykes: Games and Activities

"Hittin' the Trail" series:
Minnesota
◆Interstate State Park (ebook only)
Wisconsin
◆Barron County
◆Bayfield County
◆Burnett County (ebook only)
◆Crex Meadows Wildlife Area (ebook only)
◆Interstate State Park (ebook only)
◆Polk County (ebook only)
◆Sawyer County
National parks
◆Grand Canyon (ebook only)

ORDER THEM ONLINE AT:
dayhikingtrails.wordpress.com

WANT MORE INFO ABOUT FAMILY DAY HIKES?

Follow this book's blog, where you'll find:

Tips on day hiking with kids

Lists of great trails to hike with children

Parents' questions about
day hiking answered

Product reviews

Games and activities for the trail

News about the book series
and author

Visit online at:
hikeswithtykes.blogspot.com

www.ingramcontent.com/pod-product-compliance
Lightning Source LLC
Chambersburg PA
CBHW050531280326
41933CB00011B/1540